SPICE Up Your Life

Reflections on the Testimonies

Jay Marshall

BARCLAY PRESS

Newberg, OR 97132

SPICE Up Your Life

Reflections on the Testimonies

©2025 by Jay Marshall

Barclay Press, Inc.
Newberg, Oregon
www.barclaypress.com

All rights reserved. No part may be reproduced
for any commercial purpose by any method without
permission in writing from the copyright holder.

Printed in the United States of America

Interior design: Mareesa Fawver Moss
Cover design: Eric Muhr
Cover photo: Mae Mu via Unsplash

ISBN 978-1-59498-168-5

A remarkable book that gathers up all the bits and pieces of the Society of Friends scattered around the globe and shows us—with great understanding and a dash of Jay's trademark humor—how each one of us is intended to be a part of the whole and charged with a mission to complete.

–Ellen Michaud
author of Blessed: Living a Grateful Life and
writer-in-residence at Earlham School of Religion

Thought-provoking, entertaining, and practical! In *SPICE Up Your Life*, Jay Marshall uses fun storytelling and insightful questions to explore how traditional Quaker testimonies (or core values) can offer guidance in day-to-day living. Ranging from flat tires and dive bars to minced oaths and pimento cheese, Marshall's essays show how lofty values like simplicity, integrity, equality, and community can have down-to-earth application.

–Howard R. Macy
Professor Emeritus of Religion and Biblical Studies at George
Fox University and author of Befriending the Prophets

Read this book for Jay's stories of international travel and local eating adventures, but linger on the probing queries. Jay shares how the Quaker testimonies of peace, integrity, community, equality, and sustainability inform and shape his everyday life. His humor and curiosity, coupled with the reflective queries at the end of each chapter, encourage readers to consider how the testimonies provide meaning for each of us—particularly at this time when our society is hungry for meaning and cohesion.

–Diane Randall
Former General Secretary of Friends
Committee on National Legislation

To us who are not Quakers, Jay speaks masterfully, so much so that Quakers could look over his shoulder and learn about their treasures perhaps for the first time again. Jay is clear-eyed yet enchanting, reconnecting us with the divine in the muck and glory of everyday life. I sighed with delight, laughed out loud, and took notes to use in the years to come. This is a book to keep on the nightstand and pick up over and over again. It will help you let go, fall asleep, and rise the following day with some inexplicable strength in your step.

–Samir Selmanović, Ph.D.
Founder of TURN Community

The quest for truth has led many to seek answers in foreign places long revered, the respected writings of others both ancient and contemporary, and most often, in the populist pundits of screen and radio. It is as if truth is always "over there" and someplace removed from our place in the world. Jay Marshall calls us to the values of truthfulness in the "here and now" and in the everyday. Among Jay's stories, queries, and questions rests an invitation to consider how daily, common moments offer testimony to the larger values of life. From a yard sale to a pimento cheeseburger at Mabry's Mill, stories of practical wisdom remind readers of the sacred ordinary. Through Jay's layered writing, the reader can engage the words of a gifted storyteller, go deeper into the values unveiled with wit and intellect, and go deeper still and consider how our stories might give testimony to truthfulness. To read one story is to be inspired. To read Jay's collection of stories framed by his Quaker faith is to know of the richness of our journey and the blessing of the sacred ordinary.

–Dr. Jeffrey Carter
President, Bethany Theological Seminary

*To my wife, Judi, who continues to add spice to my life
in surprising and delightful ways.*

Table of Contents

Introduction 9
Simplicity 15
The Simple Life 17
Silence Can Be
  Good for the Soul 23
Read As You Are 29
A Tiny Town with
  a Big Taste 35
Peace 41
Flats Happen 43
Across the Valley 49
Resistance Isn't
  Futile After All 53
By the Zacchaeus Tree 57
Integrity 63
Fill My Cup 65
Fake News! 71
Not All Spam Is
  Created Equal 77
The Final Post 81
Community 87

Spiritual or Religious? 89
Lunch Anyone? 95
The Spaces Where
    We Gather 99
And Then There Was Cake 105
Equality 111
Sometimes You Are the Novelty in the Room 113
The Blessing of Corn 117
Front Door Guests 123
Fine Lines 129
Stewardship 135
Enough Already! 137
When Cussing
    Just Won't Do 145
Pimento Cheese? Really? 151
The Risk of Kindness 155
Conclusion: A Life of
    Ongoing Encounter,
    Reflection, and
    Deep Joy 161

Introduction

The word "testimony" is an intriguing word. In a courtroom context, it describes an account given by those in a position to know something about a case being adjudicated in a court of law. The individual's knowledge or experience contributes to efforts that will create a narrative without which determining the truth would be impossible. In the context of faith, however, the word testimony is used to describe the story someone tells about their life, usually involving God's intervention in a profound way. Depending on the personality and the context, it may be uttered in words barely audible or delivered with dramatic fanfare and shouting surrounded by an amen chorus. Either way, in sharing their experiences, those giving testimony serve as witnesses to the divine work in their lives and, by extension, suggest that others consider their own spiritual condition.

With Friends, in particular, "testimony" is a word used to describe convictions or values that have risen to the level of truthfulness in the context of the corporate worship experience. As such, they provide guidance on the quality or philosophy of life to be undertaken and influence what are considered acceptable as appropriate practices. Like the North Star, testimonies provide a reference point that helps us navigate life's journey.

In their early stages, testimonies helped Friends answer the question, "How shall we live in light of our religious experiences?" Testimonies also helped them define and distinguish themselves among other religious groups evolving during this period. Probably no group begins by thinking they must hammer out a list of dos and don'ts, even though religions seem notorious for creating them over time. But meaningful worship has a way of transforming every human being.

Encounters with the Spirit of the living God shine a light deep into our hearts where we hold the deepest of values, loves, and biases. Some of those will be embraced and uplifted, but others will likely be broken over time. For example, in worship, perhaps you experience a feeling of love and sense your place in the wider creation. In the process, you come to realize that hierarchies that devalue others, even as they protect your sense of security, can no longer be endorsed. In fact, this could very well be the first step toward embracing equality at the level of testimony—a truth intended to affect social order and interactions in which love and respect resist temptations to exploit, oppress, or ignore others.

Or perhaps, in the quietness of worship, you are surprised to revisit old memories of conflicts or even violence. There, as the light shines upon them, you may experience remorse for your role in the conflict—particularly if you were the aggressor and recognize that such attitudes and actions are both harmful and contradictory to the precepts of the faith you profess to embrace.

Every life is anchored to some set of values. Although some lives may appear to drift aimlessly without a care in the world, even they have likely set a course that is motivated and supported by the values and preferences that most strongly influence their perspective. Many of those standards are planted within the individual during their formative years, influenced by those around us. But as we mature and personal preferences develop, we have an opportunity to reshape or revise them.

The potential choices are numerous. Shall we choose love or hate? Will our default tendency be to generosity or stinginess? Shall we prefer equality or our own superiority? Might we commit to peacefulness when we encounter others, or do we adopt hostility as our leading impulse? There are a multitude of options available. Fortunately, however, societies find it possible to agree on a few values that, generally speaking, allow the creation of a standard of ethics or a moral code.

Though we may claim some of these standards are self-evident, I think it is more honest to acknowledge that they are arbitrary. They form around ideas and practices that appeal to the group. If we are a peace-loving group, then an endorsement of peace is probable; on the other hand, if we are smitten with a "to the victor go the spoils" mentality, we can expect more allowances to be made for feisty behavior. To further solidify these choices once they are made, the group will imbue them with power from on high. That is to say, they are endorsed by whatever ultimate authorities we recognize, be it the Divine, the head of the clan, or the state.

I recall the disorientation experienced in my first church history class. Several beliefs and practices that had been represented as divinely mandated were, in fact, the result of decisions made by councils of men. That they may have been well-intentioned did not diminish the loss of respect I had for several of those beliefs and practices because their origin and authority was different than what I had been taught. As troubling as that was, it was not without value, for it also freed me to think through those items for myself and determine which, if any, would continue to claim my allegiance.

I confess that I don't know when or how all of the choices are made in the course of someone's life, but I do know that we each live with their consequences. Increasingly, in this generation, I hear numerous individuals clamoring for consistency between their values and their commitments. That is to say, they want to spend their work lives on projects that make a difference and align with their core convictions. They want to devote ample time to families and friends who matter most in their networks of support. They desire time to reconnect with their own dreams as a way of rejuvenating, enjoying, and contributing to their life and their communities.

It is precisely here that attention to the idea of testimonies bears fruit. Early Friends possessed a deep dedication to their community as part of their collective commitment to a faith that questioned, discarded, and reframed much of traditional seventeenth-century Christian beliefs. From their corporate worship experience and the trials of life, there emerged a consensus that a life aligned with the leadings of God's Spirit would demonstrate a commitment to personal integrity, peace, equality, and simplicity. These became known as testimonies, demonstrating the veracity of Friends commitment to their interpretation of truthfulness. As life is not static, neither is faithfulness. Over time, community and stewardship were identified as testimonies as well, leading to the mnemonic device SPICES as a means of remembering them. And as should be expected, occasionally, calls are made for new additions to the group.

Among those who embraced them in the past, the testimonies might be visibly evident through such things as plain speech (thees and thous), as a means of refusing to acknowledge social standing. For a period, Friends adopted a certain style of dress as an expression of simplicity, once again setting themselves apart from the prominent fashion and patterns adopted by society. The testimony of equality influenced views on the role of women in society and encouraged participation in the abolition movement. As inspiring as many of these historical examples are, a twenty-first-century seeker of truth may find themselves grappling with two important questions: Are these testimonies ones with which we wish to align ourselves? If so, how, in fact, might these testimonies find expression in our lives? A third question warrants mention as well: If these testimonies do not resonate with us, what will we choose in their place?

As difficult as those ruminations may initially appear, they are engaged more easily if we simply take time for personal reflection on our lives. What are the causes that matter? What are the things that cause us grief? Where do we find inspiration and joy? My suspicion is we already know many of the answers to these questions. If we haven't taken time to acknowledge them thus far in our lives, they will likely lay buried deep within our hearts, waiting for discovery. Once we can name the values that matter, we better know what to nurture and what to tamp down in our own lives, and are better positioned to make the most of the time we have.

This book invites your reflection on key themes that have been important among Friends, but it will also speak to a wider swath of the population as well because their merit has been proven countless times among those who have attempted to embrace and honor them for centuries.

The essays in this book are not deep dives into history as a means of teaching us yet again what we once knew. Rather, they observe and reflect upon experiences in life that, once noticed, raise questions, make connections, and nudge us to ponder their nuances and implications. Once in the habit of inward reflection and even introspection, we can quickly recognize the testimonies we are giving even if we've never noticed them before.

Simplicity

The Freedom of an Uncluttered Life

Rather than "What is easiest?" Simplicity asks, "What is most important in life?" Once answered, it works to winnow away all that complicates or distracts from giving our utmost attention to the things that matter.

The Simple Life

For much of our married life, my wife and I had two households. In grad school, one was an apartment within walking distance of the Duke campus, while the other was the home provided by the Friends meeting where I served as pastor during that time. Later, the parsonage provided as part of Judi's compensation by the United Methodist Church was our main residence, and the second was a house we were buying for the day when she retired. I joked that it also served as "bishop insurance," meaning that, if the bishop ever appointed Judi to a place she did not want to go, we had an easy housing option.

Thankfully, that was never an issue. But one consequence of Judi's decision to retire a few years ago was that we reduced from two households to one. Honestly, it was a relief to be able to do so, but we were faced with a pressing question. What to do with all the duplications we owned? Two microwave ovens, excess lamps, dishes, and more.

In East Central Indiana, the obvious solution to this overstocked situation is a yard sale, where one arranges one's goods on the front lawn and invites strangers to rifle through those belongings while insisting that a nearly new toaster is worth no more than fifty cents rather than the outrageous one-dollar price tag attached to it. Yard sales are such a cultural fixture that small towns in our area coordinate to offer a weekend long event along US Highway 40. It creates a big obstacle for those who simply want to use the highway for its intended purpose of transportation.

Judi and I set our own date and advertised the coming event. In the interim, we sorted and organized our items. Finally, we waited. In what must be the antithesis of arriving fashionably late, bargain shoppers began arriving a good hour before the posted start time. And there was plenty to see. Reducing two households down to one, enhanced by twenty-plus years of accumulation produced, shall we say, a healthy inventory. Fortunately, we had a large front yard.

This exercise proved to be a spiritual aha moment. It began when the first customer sauntered through the aisles and innocently said, "Wow. This is a lot of stuff. How many families are participating in this yard sale?"

"Just one," I answered.

"How large is the family?" he pressed.

On the off chance that customer service was important, even at yard sales, I responded politely, "Just the two of us."

A few minutes later, another visitor with hands on her hips and mouth agape asked, "Is this an estate sale?"

"No ma'am," I responded. "Moving it all outside nearly killed us both, but we all still had a pulse as of this morning."

If those two were like ghosts of Christmas past and present, my third ghost arrived in the form of a friend who came over on her lunch hour and exclaimed, "Wow, is this all your stuff?" Being the smart aleck I am, I said, "Why no, we have more in the house that is not for sale. If you don't see what you're looking for here, we can go inside to look through the rest!"

Honestly, their comments were merely salt in the wound. The whole preparation process had left me aghast at how much stuff we had accumulated. Even the word "stuff" implies such a wide range as to defy precise, descriptive categories. It hints at being too much, as when one is "stuffed" at the end of a meal. I have heard others express a similar response during their own spring cleaning efforts, so perhaps you understand what I was going through. Some duplication was understandable given the need to furnish two homes over the years, but this experience was calling me to deeper reflection. How did this happen? Why had I not noticed?

Intellectually, I know I am more than my material possessions. My value is not enhanced by the car I drive or the logo on my clothing or how much I own. I recognize the seduction cast by our consumer-oriented culture that regularly parades nonessential, if not useless, gadgets as though life is incomplete without them. I would describe very few of my possessions as frivolous; still, accumulation without reflection or critique is an easy habit to develop, creating cluttered homes and complex relationships with the items we choose to claim as our own. It can be difficult to liberate one's self from it all.

Interestingly enough, early Quakers named simplicity as a worthy practice for the spiritually inclined. Though there is evidence this was not a fully embraced commitment, the idea continues to circulate as a desirable quality of the spiritual life. Frankly, simplicity has suffered from widespread neglect through the years. Lack of simplicity does not make many short lists of sins to be forgiven or habits to be changed.

Perhaps part of this is due to the general connotation of the word itself. "Simple" often equates with "easy." In some cases, that which comes easily may not be worth having or at least not immediately trustworthy. My guess is that sentiment was coined and marketed by those who sported a strong work ethic.

The fact that the word "simpleton" is used to describe foolish or gullible individuals may discourage a stampede toward simplicity as well. Who wants to attempt to live down that reputation?

Simple sometimes implies "less advanced" or "less complicated." While we may cringe at the idea of being considered "less advanced," especially if that somehow is interpreted as less cultured or less capable, "less complicated" can be desirable. I appreciate phone apps that make complex computer functions manageable for the technologically untrained. I like subway maps that can be understood by visitors and tourists (are you listening, New York City?). And if less complicated means "less baggage," then I really appreciate simple, less complicated relationships. If I could add a day to my life for every incorrect assumption or interpretation others have made about something I've said, not said, done, or not done based on the baggage they lug through life, I might well outlive Methuselah.

But what might simple mean as a spiritual practice or attitude in life that is not burdened by negative implications? For better or worse, we often evaluate simplicity by material measures like price and quantity—buying twenty-dollar sneakers instead of three-hundred-dollar pair or owning one pair of jeans rather than a dozen. Those measures are important, but I doubt they are the only and perhaps not even the primary determination of simplicity. Things like the quality of goods purchased and the means by which the items were created are important as well. Multiple levels of corporate ownership and numerous steps between producer and consumer make it difficult to know the full details and consequences of our choices. Even when available, those facts are often overlooked in a system that depends on reoccurring business or that awards contracts to lowest bids without ensuring equality of proposals. I shake my head when delivery people tell me the average lifespan of their appliance is five years, knowing those of my grandparents sometimes lasted decades. Choosing to purchase cheap garments that last one season at best rather than paying more for clothes that last for years may be a case of frugality or of economic necessity, but is not necessarily an example of simplicity.

What if we were to begin by considering that simplicity is not a mandate for a sacrifice of quality and instead turn our attention to quantity? Here, we may discover that our purchasing habits are off the rails. Judging by the number of antique shops around the country and the popularity of storage unit rentals, I think society has made its peace with at least a four-tiered system of "stuff." Level one consists of items we truly treasure that stay at home where we can see them, touch them, even be inspired by them. For me, beyond those items with practical functions, these consist mainly of photos or travel mementos that remind me of happy experiences. What are yours?

Level two includes things we never use and do not miss but cannot bear to release because we might need them one day. These are stored in attics, basements, and rented storage units. If it has been in a box unused for five years, it is not a high priority item, though as soon as I get rid of it, I will need it the next week. Or at least, that rationale helps justify hanging on to multiple claw hammers or three partially complete sets of drill bits.

A few of us utilize level three. It consists of things we no longer want but believe others might be willing to purchase. These wind up in antique stores or posted on the likes of eBay. But until someone hands over the cash, it still counts as part of the volume of stuff we cannot release.

The fourth level is reserved for things we are not sure anyone would buy, but since one person's trash can be another's treasure, those items can be donated. The fact it can be considered as recycling means we can dispense of it and still feel good about letting it go.

Imagine how much less space we would need or how much less trash we would have if a commitment to simplicity resulted in buyer constraint. While it would declutter our personal space and positively affect our cash flow, I confess I do not know how it would impact an economy that depends on wanton purchasing habits. It may be a risk we are not willing to take.

Building on this thread, if simplicity does not sacrifice quality but does commit to more responsible decisions that declutter our space, one could ask if simplicity is merely concerned with external clutter. As Quakers learned, a preoccupation with the simplicity of external trappings could lead to such obsessions as what constitutes a suitable fabric and weave of cloth used for garments or what is the acceptable height for tombstones. I wonder if there isn't also an internal clutter that complicates our lives? I have witnessed it in the exhausting complexity that results from over-committed schedules. I have faced it in the busyness that ultimately makes us strangers in our most intimate relationships, including our relationship to ourselves. Many of us know some variation of that experience. Perhaps we work multiple jobs to make ends meet. Or we are overextended through our passionate volunteerism for causes we love. Possibly it results from the rhythm of the life we have chosen, which requires two-hour commutes in each direction sandwiched around an eight-hour day so that we are burning the proverbial candle at both ends. Our interior space can be overcrowded by these commitments. Our attention can be splintered by competing demands. As a consequence, we slowly but surely lose sight of our inner core that keeps us centered and accountable to our values.

My hunch is that simplicity is best rooted in the interior space where we notice our values and desires. Planted and nurtured there, the seed of simplicity tempers our attitudes and practices. There it gives life to a disposition, a posture that knows none of us can do all or be all. It understands that most of us need less than we think and that richness arises from relationships and experiences more than things. It has some calm understanding of the power of enough, an invigorating force that allows us to relax and trust and love and simply be present wherever we are.

Simple may not be so easy after all.

Query for contemplation: In an effort to meet the various demands on your life, have you overcommitted your time or overaccumulated possessions? If so, can you imagine a first step that will move you toward a simpler life? How will you begin?

Silence Can Be Good for the Soul

It had been a busy day, full of crowds and traffic. It was not anything like Los Angeles rush hour or I-95 holiday travel, but one's idea of congestion is usually conditioned by what has become familiar or normal. Some days, it is tough for me just to poke along for a half mile behind three Amish buggies on shoulder-less Indiana county roads with enough obstructions that I cannot pass them. This day as I drove home, a radio announcer, offering a bit of pastoral commentary to listeners, said empathetically, "We just want you to know that you are not alone." My exhausted, introverted self said, "I know. And that is precisely the problem!" Loneliness is no laughing matter, to be sure, but neither is the lack of solitude. Whether via a solitary lifestyle, a daily practice, or periodic respites that provide a break from the overload of stimuli packing much of our lives, a bit of silence can be good for the soul.

To be sure, silence can be tricky, especially around other people. Some may sense it is the "cold shoulder" and wonder what they have done to merit that response. Or it may be perceived as disinterest toward them, which is not a message we want to send to friends and loved ones. The possible misinterpretations made by others are countless. In a society that has come to believe that "aliveness" is somehow connected to busyness, talk, and external stimuli, silence looks like a stranger among us. On occasion, I have watched with amazement the animated conversations in a room bursting with loud talk and booming energy and asked myself, "What on earth do all these people have to talk about with such enthusiasm?" This is especially true if this happens over breakfast! (Okay. So in addition to smart aleck and introvert, occasionally I manifest a dash of the curmudgeon as well.)

For some, silence is like beer or coffee or unsweetened tea—it is an acquired taste and requires a period of adjustment before it becomes palatable or something to seek out frequently. One weekend soon after my wife and I were married, we were spending the night in the parsonage of the Quaker meeting I served while attending seminary. It was located in an idyllic rural North Carolina setting surrounded by woods and pasture. Shortly after we had turned off the lights, and I had closed my eyes to sleep, she whispered, "It is so quiet out here. Could we turn on a fan to create a little noise?"

Personally, being silent is one of my favorite states of being. Maybe that is my natural disposition or the effect of spending many childhood hours alone while doing farm chores. For whatever reason, I am comfortable hanging out in quietness and find it to be many things but never empty and void. It seems as necessary to me as a charging station is to an electric car.

For starters, silence provides moments for reflection. Many of us experience life as a treadmill that reinforces the idea that we are part of the proverbial "rat race." Doing more and doing it faster are presented as major rules of the game. Time away, if you get it, is often viewed as an escape that helps avoid exhaustion, but even this is sacrificed in the wild dash to win in the human race. It is true that life and schedules are complicated, and one cannot actually make more time; but I advocate for creating time to put up your feet and sit back and dare to recount the day. Relive a conversation that affirmed you, or dream of the future you want or the community you intend to help create. Silence is an opportunity to explore ideas, possibilities, or puzzles that make sense of life's quandaries or prepare us for things yet to come.

Silence of this quality is more than just an opportunity for imagination and entertaining hopes. At times, it will also invite us on quiet walks through deserted places or favorite memories that remind us of heartaches and sadness that still linger, though in muted levels compared to what was once felt. Even these are not to be avoided, for they help us continue to refine the lessons being learned through life's difficult moments where we learned how deeply pain can sear to the core but also came to know the reality of our own resilience. In an odd sort of way, cemeteries illustrate this for me. Cemeteries are some of the most silent places we ever encounter. Within their gates, they house what remains of once vibrant lives whose voices have fallen silent, now marked by stones bearing a variety of symbols often selected as clues to how the deceased wanted to be remembered. They trigger the contemplation of past loves whose memories live on or perhaps of our own mortality. There, in the silence, we find space and time to remember, to relive, to refocus.

Imagine a similar practice outside the cemetery focused not on loves lost but on hopes still dreamed or issues yet to be tackled or hurts needing to be healed. When we are swept along in a continual stream of interruptions and distracting noise, it is difficult to notice those inner seeds that can only germinate when attention is given to the testimony they bear within us. Tending to these is part of the secret to vitality.

In silence, we encounter more than the opportunity to explore and reflect upon a range of interesting topics. It grants us space to hear ourselves weigh in on things that matter to our health and heart. We most easily learn the things we value, the commitments we are willing to make, and the changes that must be made when we dare to be silent long enough to hear our deepest self.

Those who know me are aware that I chose to retire from a position I held for twenty years. It was work that inspired me. It opened opportunities and expanded possibilities for others. It contributed to a sense of purpose and meaning for the life I lived and the call to ministry that I answered. I loved that work and could have continued on that path if I had chosen to do so. Only it was becoming clear to me that my work in that role was possibly wrapping up. One day as I sat in silence listening for the truth that was in me related to my work, I heard myself say, "I don't want to do this anymore." It was surprising yet believable. It gave the final vote in a decision I knew was all but complete.

I often view silence as an opportunity to turn inward. Without doubt, that is my instinct. But, like coming to a fork in the road, there is another route to enjoy from time to time. One can silently open one's self to the surrounding world. I find that, some days, it takes more effort to pay attention to my surroundings, but it is well worth it. Become an observer. A listener. A witness. See colors or smiles; witness fear or injustice. Most would not have been noticed had silence not disengaged me from other things so that I could be available in that moment to see what was present before me. Silence not only calms the noise; it contributes to openness and attentiveness that notices inspiration and opportunity that may have otherwise been missed.

And there is one other grand discovery to be experienced within the silence: the Divine is a frequent guest who meets us there. It is a practice and experience described in certain psalms: "Be still, and know that I am God" (Psalm 46:10) or "For God alone my soul waits in silence" (Psalm 62:1). Quakers have long advocated for silence as a means of communion with God. Whether in private or in community, it is an opportunity to intentionally wait, and having stilled one's self, to listen for what rises within us. One of my favorite reminders of this comes from Thomas Kelly's *Testament of Devotion*:

> Deep within us all there is an amazing inner sanctuary of the soul, a holy place, a Divine Center, a speaking Voice, to which we may continuously return. Eternity is at our hearts, pressing upon our time-torn lives, warming us with intimations of an astounding destiny, calling us home unto Itself. Yielding to these persuasions, gladly committing ourselves in body and

soul, utterly and completely, to the Light Within, is the beginning of true life.[1]

One of the great gifts of silence is the reminder of Divine accompaniment. Apparently, it is true after all—we are not alone, and at least in certain circumstances, that is a good and useful thing.

Query for Contemplation: What are your practices for breaking apart from life's chaos for periodic reprieves in which you find simple paths to solitude and quietness where you most easily hear the Divine?

---

[1] Thomas, Kelly, *A Testament of Devotion* (San Francisco: Harper and Brothers, 1941), pp. 9–10.

Read As You Are

"Be careful what you ask for!" Cautionary advice like this statement was liberally sprinkled throughout my childhood. It was often offered as a veiled threat that promised unpleasant consequences lay ahead if certain things didn't change. Warning or not, those words conveyed valuable information about the importance of being mindful of the things we say. Once released into the world, they take on a life of their own, inviting interpretations we may not have intended and responses we may not desire. Perhaps that is why my mind sometimes wonders about intent, the meaning beneath the surface of things said. Was our brain even paying attention when the sentence was being formulated?

In my youth, I frequently heard the statement, "Well, don't rush off." I don't know about elsewhere, but in our part of the South, that was a standard response said to guests who indicated they intended to leave. Dinner ended hours ago. The card game was completed. Rich conversation flowed throughout the evening. A good time was had by all. It was time to go. Even so, it was nearly impossible to get out the door without hearing those words. Sometimes, it meant just what it said—"The time together has been enjoyable, and we hate to see it end." Other times, I have heard it slip from my own lips before I even realized it was on its way out, as though it were part of a departure ritual. I've said it on occasions when I could barely contain my yawns or keep my eyes open.

Honestly, the last thing I wanted in that moment was for the guest to stay one minute longer. Whether the visit lasted thirty minutes or a few hours, Southern hospitality seemed to demand such a response. Perhaps it is part thank you and part standing invitation to return, a permanent welcome if you will. But what if the ones leaving took the comment at face value and sat back down to stay a while longer? We'd survive, I suppose, but it isn't what we had in mind. As the saying goes, "Be careful what you ask for."

Another comment ripe for disaster is, "Come in and make yourself at home." It is the kind of welcome meant to put a guest at ease, but it is a risky thing to say without knowing how that person behaves in their own home. I take off my shoes as soon as I walk in the door at my house, but I'm reluctant to do that in someone else's abode without an invitation. I remember a development call several years ago when a new colleague accompanied me on his first visit. As soon as we stepped inside the house of our donor, my colleague took off his shoes. No one said anything, but the look on our host's face left no doubt that she was surprised. Later when I asked what possessed him to do that, my colleague said it was standard practice where he was from. To do otherwise would be rude.

On the TV sitcom, *The Goldbergs*, the father drops his pants when he arrives home at the end of the day, leaves them on the floor by the front door, and marches in his tighty-whities directly toward his favorite chair by the television. Others make themselves at home by putting their feet on the coffee table. Ottomans and recliners are made for that purpose, but I suppose we are programmed to make use of what is available. All of those may be fine in one's own home, but is any of that really what is being offered by the statement: "Make yourself at home"? We all have at-home habits that allow us to get comfortable and relax but that if practiced in someone else's home might cause discomfort. It is a sincere statement to welcome others into our space, but again, "Be careful what you ask for." Su casa may not be mi casa after all.

This line of thought was most recently rekindled when I noticed a church sign that belongs in this category of good-intentioned expressions of welcome. It strikes me as one that means well but isn't as true as we would like to believe. It read: "Welcome. Come as you are." That led me first to wonder, how else would a person come except as they are? Certainly, we can pretend to be something we are not, but can we really ever leave who we are behind? It could be argued that church is the one place where a person feels pressured to put on airs, dress to the nines (well, not anymore), be what we've heard God wants us to be, and not show our true colors because "as we are" could never meet the standard for admission.

If that is the case, perhaps guests and strangers need encouragement to come as they are, and the regulars need a reminder that it is okay to do so as well. The statement is likely intended as welcoming and invitational, which is a positive, but I have been around long enough to know there are usually limits to this sentiment.

Even the most universal welcomes, at least the ones I have seen, have boundaries beyond which the receiving group can't extend themselves. I've known things like ethnicity, political ideology, and theology to be dealbreakers in the reception of seekers looking for a new community. Or more challenging, what if "coming as you are" means as a kleptomaniac or an arsonist or a person prone to violence or abuse?

It is a challenge. Being welcoming and inclusive is not as simple as propping open the door and saying, "Ya'll come." Unless those differences can remain nonissues, then the welcome statement is at best incomplete (as in, "come as you are, and we'll help make you over") and at worst untruthful. More honest, perhaps, was another church's invitation: "Come as you are. You can change inside." That at least makes clear that a larger agenda or set of community standards are behind the welcome. Yep. Be careful what you ask for. And perhaps, just as importantly, be careful of what you say yes to. Not all welcomes are equal.

Exchanges like these carry me into the realm of simple conversation, though some days, very little about it seems to be easy. Apparently, it is often difficult to say what we mean, so we employ euphemisms (for instance, "I lost my husband" usually doesn't mean the couple got separated at the supermarket, though it might) or phrases that make sense to you but no one else. For instance, what does "that tickles the daylights out of me" really mean? Even Google doesn't seem to know, but you might hear it from me on occasion. Then there are statements that only convey the more palatable portion of what we mean:

- "I *hate* drama!" Generally that means, "Look out because there is about to be some."
- "No worries." Mmm, most likely a bit of preoccupation is on the way. Even if it is not yours, it may cause you a bit of strife.
- "It's okay." It's probably not, even if everyone involved wants it to be. At our house, when used to describe a dish or meal, "it's okay" is as enthused an endorsement as earning an F in a pass/fail class.

Language can be complicated. Even if you master the rules of grammar, there is no guarantee you will communicate clearly. Idioms, slang, and dysfunctions cloud the message. Tone and intent shade meaning, which brings us back to phrases that mean what they say but may not say exactly what we mean.

Rarely, if ever, is anyone intending harm or deceit in these responses. The desired good lives in subtle tension with truthfulness. Why is it so difficult to operate with careful candor in which we clearly articulate what we mean while making an effort to appreciate and not offend the other?

Quakers sometimes talk about "plain speech." I have referred to the use of "thee" and "thou" as a means of abstaining from socially imposed hierarchy. Among contemporary Friends, it more often describes frank, direct talk that attempts to get right to the point. In my opinion, some use it as permission to be rude, bossy, or just plain meddlesome. Still, within the idea lives a seed for direct communication that could express appreciation or extend welcome without confusion, false promises, or erroneous expectations.

I'd love to see the world make a concerted effort to speak clearly and plainly, especially about things that matter. We may discover we're more appreciated than we knew or less welcome than we thought. But at least we would know where we stand and could plan our next move accordingly. Then again, I'd best be careful what I ask for. So read as long as you want. I'd hate for you to rush off.

Query for Contemplation: Do you find it difficult to speak clearly and directly with others? If you are able, are your words characterized by care and tactfulness?

A Tiny Town with a Big Taste

The Appalachian Mountains boast breathtaking beauty, whether it be their towering trees, playful streams, or alluring skylines viewed from a deck overlooking a majestic valley. Villages and small towns are sprinkled throughout this territory, quietly minding their own business until word of their attractiveness leaks out, and streets swell with crowds eager to get in on the fun.

West Jefferson, North Carolina, is one of those little gems. Founded in 1909, it was once a stop on the Norfolk and Western Railroad and home of the only cheese factory in the Southeast. With a population of around 1,300, according to the last census, it's the kind of place that invites you to get lost wandering its streets even though it is pretty much impossible to do so.

One of the things you'll find here is a little restaurant called Black Jack's Bar and Grill. With a name like that, it sounds better suited for a casino or a pirate's ship, but in this little town, it's a happening eatery. Founded by a Romanian-born woman named Virginia, in 2008, it has since passed down to her son who continues to infuse old country spices into his cooking. One of my sisters introduced me to the town and the restaurant while I was visiting her a couple summers ago.

Black Jack's claims to have been voted the best burger in town. With a population of 1,300, there aren't likely many competitors for that honor, so I don't know if that title really brings much distinction. But I will say the burger I ordered gets a blue ribbon in my book. I chose the Black Jack's burger. As for condiments, it features some old reliables like lettuce, tomato, and mayo. The addition of bacon supercharges the flavor. It brings a nice pepper jack cheese to the party as well, which I always enjoy because of its spicy kick. I'm a sucker for a little heat. One favorite photo tucked away in our vacation pictures shows me red-faced, sweating, and obviously happy while devouring a pickled jalapeño at a restaurant during a trip through the Copper Canyon in Mexico. However, it was the new kid on the cheeseburger block that made the Black Jack burger a standout: a nice full slice of pineapple, perhaps half an inch thick, grilled to complement the burger with a hint of smoky sweetness.

To be honest, I've always liked good pineapple. This fruit has never been better than the time I stood in a pineapple field in Costa Rica and enjoyed it freshly picked, then sliced up with a machete and served from the tailgate of a truck. Chalk up part of that pleasure to location and context, but it sure helps when a person knows how to determine a pineapple's ripeness and can pick it at its peak. I was like a kid in a candy store that day.

Pineapple makes a surprisingly good addition to a cheeseburger. Its sweet flavor blends with its condiment companions in a way that is both distinct yet complementary. It was the kind of bite that reduced me to moans as I savored it. I even closed my eyes while chewing, as though blocking out all distractions increased its flavor. I know that probably makes as much sense as turning down the radio so you can see better when driving in a rain storm, but I guess both strategies help us to focus and concentrate.

To recap, here is the description as listed on the Black Jack's menu: Beef patty with pepper jack cheese, grilled pineapple, bacon, lettuce, tomato, and mayo.

It is not uncommon after a dining experience like that to try and recreate it back home. Those efforts rarely measure up to the original experience. We have a corn soup recipe from an Egyptian chef that, while very good, never tastes quite the same as it did the time he prepared it. That wasn't the case in this instance. After enjoying this burger so much, I served grilled pineapple the next time we had friends over for a cookout. It was a huge success! Even now, when I recall that burger, my taste buds salivate a little.

I confess I am a bit surprised by this. Pineapple was not unknown or unappreciated prior to tasting it on this burger. It was a simple addition—creative, mind you—but simple. Perhaps it even qualifies as bold or courageous if some doubted pineapple's place on the menu at all or its ability to make a contribution paired with these other items, but mostly it is just a simple choice.

It brings to mind the lyrics of the old Shaker tune, "Simple Gifts":

'Tis the gift to be simple, 'tis the gift to be free,
'Tis the gift to come down where we ought to be,
And when we find ourselves in the place just right,
'Twill be in the valley of love and delight.

Those who sing the song often resonate with the idea that simple things—be they gifts, treasures, or lifestyles—often have a sense of "rightness" that aligns us with our truer, deeper purpose, freeing us from the trappings of misperceptions, overcommitments, and misplaced values. That is not to say everything can or needs to be simple, but there are times when it is indeed just right.

Choosing a simple option, even if it is a novel one, may be the insight this cheeseburger recipe offers. In a world where binary language and algorithms increasingly drive so much of our interactions, even small tasks are supported by complexity behind the scenes. It is good to be reminded occasionally that complexity is not a prerequisite for value, joy, or happiness. How many times have you seen children opt to play with a cardboard box rather than the gift it originally contained? Or experienced your mood transformed simply by spending a little time outdoors?

As many learned during the practice of sheltering at home, simple gifts and pleasures are within our reach and have the capacity to nourish and renew us. Remove a couple of hours of playing Road Warrior from your daily schedule or spending all your time rushing through unnecessary appointments or shuttling family members around town and suddenly you find yourself with a slower pace. You have time to devote to quality purposes. I have heard from a growing number of people that they and their families are rediscovering this (and each other) together.

As we learn to appreciate simple things, we become more comfortable sharing simple gifts and gestures. These carry their own power to influence deeply. Part of the power of the simple gift is its ability to generate surprise in the new combinations we encounter because of it. Pineapple itself is tasty enough. But the simple addition of it to the texture of a grilled burger or the saltiness of bacon or the picante contribution of the pepper jack cheese introduces something new. Each one on its own has a splendid and unique flavor, but together, new profiles are created that are not possible alone.

Sometimes, simple choices allow for combinations not yet sampled but eagerly accepted once they are known. This is true for more than just cheeseburgers. Those combinations can create new recipes, friendships, and alliances. They introduce new tastes, possibilities, strengths, and solutions. They can cross neighborhoods, economic class, religious differences—all sorts of sociological complexities that, however purposeful they may be, also discourage us from sampling other combinations that would delight us if we ever had the opportunity to experience them.

Simple things, be they gifts, choices, or gestures—don't underestimate their power. And if you happen to pass through this tiny town with big taste, have lunch at Black Jack's. Tell them Jay sent you. They'll have no idea who you're talking about and probably won't give you a discount, but you'll have a conversation starter. And they'll still serve you a mouthwatering cheeseburger!

Query for Contemplation: What options do you have for making simpler choices that could enrich your joy while reducing your life's complexity?

Toward a Testimony of Simplicity
Questions for Further Reflection

1. What obligations or distractions most interfere with my attentiveness to the presence of the Divine in my life?
2. Where do I spend most of my time? Am I present and invested with the people and purposes that matter most to me?
3. Am I able to say "no" when demands on my time or resources place me in positions that are untenable with my convictions?
4. Are my purchases based on need or driven by advertising? Am I most influenced by quality and value or status?
5. Are there segments of my life that consistently overwhelm me? How can I simplify my life with regard to their impact?

Peace

Clearing Pathways; Building Bridges

At its best, peace is less about eliminating threats and conquering discord and more about disarming the distress caused by our differences. In effect, it takes away the occasion for war. Imagine a world where our commonality eliminates the urge to hate rather than love or to conquer rather than coexist, and you will have caught a glimpse of peace as a testimony.

Flats Happen

Someone else's nail winds up in your tire, and before you can say "psssst," the road of life gifts you with a flat. It rarely occurs at a convenient time. It often happens on the narrowest road with the least amount of shoulder room available or the busiest of interstate exits. Beyond the inconvenience, the most difficult part of the ordeal can be remembering exactly where in the car the manufacturer decided to hide the jack. Inside the trunk? In a side storage compartment over the wheel well? Beneath the front seat? Fortunately, my last tire ordeal was a slow leak rather than a blowout, allowing me to drive to the repair center for service rather than sweat through a roadside change.

Exiled to the customer service lounge at the tire center, I waited for the repair to be completed. Waiting areas are a nice idea, but the experience can be like a cross between a dating set-up and prison. You never know with whom you're being set up, how long you have to pretend you're enjoying it, or how quickly you'll be released. Sitting at the mercy of a blaring TV to which no one was listening and a group of fellow customers who were engrossed in an animated conversation, it was my intent to ignore the entire racket and pass the time.

Despite our best efforts, some voices simply cannot be tuned out, having a volume or tone that refuses to be denied. One of those was holding forth a few chairs away from where I sat that day. It was from him that I overhead these words: "When I go to church, I want to learn something, and I want to be encouraged so that I can go out and face this nasty world." This statement was part of an explanation of why he had recently stopped attending one church and chosen another. More honestly, it was about his dissatisfaction with that particular pastor, but this version presented the matter in a far nobler fashion. His departure was not an impulse decision. He spoke with the minister in advance, explained what was lacking in the worship experience, gave advice on what the minister could do to improve the situation, and allowed a few weeks to see if things changed before departing.

I appreciated this person's desire that learning be part of a worship experience. I admired the fact that, in the midst of his dissatisfaction, he hadn't impulsively "taken his toys and gone home," leaving behind a mystery for others to waste countless hours trying to solve. Instead, he'd voiced his frustrations to his minister because, in his words, he needed help dealing with life.

Still, something about the exchange troubled me. With time, I realized the disturbing part of those comments was the description of this world as "nasty." As used that day, it sounded disgusting and dismissive. What would be the determining factor in awarding a negative label like that to our experience of life? I suspect that characterization was likely formed either by teaching the person received over time or his interpretation of life's experiences.

For whatever reason, much of Christianity ignores statements in Genesis that God blessed all creation and called it good. Instead, it prefers to give nearly unlimited power to the idea that humanity's propensity for self-centeredness creates a sinful condition that places a giant pause on any discussions of goodness. When it comes to the topic of sin, preachers can be like pigs in a mud hole—they love to wallow in it to the point that every sermon is covered in mud: what it looks like, what it feels like, how it cakes as it dries, categories of mud, how impossible it is to stay out of it or remove it, and so on. Thanks to this fascination with mud, if there were a Cliffs Note for Christianity, under the section on creation, in the words of South Park's Mr. Mackey, it would likely say, "The world is bad, m'kay?" Tarnished thanks to humanity's depravity. It's a treacherous place for the faithful, so be wary—be in the world but not of it. It's nasty. It is that simple. That's a common viewpoint, to be sure, but is it accurate? Is it the whole story?

If my waiting area buddy didn't adopt this point of view from previous teachings shared with him, then perhaps this perception of a "nasty" world was formed by his life's experiences. After all, they are extremely influential. What if he grew up as an unwanted child, ignored at home or passed around in the system, never feeling like he was loved or belonged? Or if for reasons he never understood, he was always identified as being one of the outcasts or underachievers in his school? What if he was passed over for college admission or a scholarship that would have changed the paths available in life? Or perhaps a few bad decisions derailed his dreams, and he's been stuck in an unwanted situation for all these however many years.

Possibly none of that is true—he could be well-satisfied with his own success, except for reading the morning headlines day after day. There, each morning, he receives a report of just how nasty the world is. Corporate greed extorts America. Drug cartels create havoc in the territories they claim. Nations threaten one another's sovereignty. Another story about police violence raises questions about the trustworthiness of the law. Scenarios like those paint a grim picture. Maybe you could even call it "nasty."

I may not want to label this world in that way, but I can't say there aren't reasons why someone could draw that conclusion. This may be one of those cases where we find what we're looking for and can support either position with ample anecdotes or a smattering of data that reinforce our decision. The truth of the matter is that we each have to make our peace with the world around us. Like whether we'll love, tolerate, or mostly ignore our neighbor. Or whether we'll approach one another with a positive outlook and hope for a good connection or begin each encounter with reserve and suspicion, taking a "guilty until proven innocent" kind of approach. I know that once I assign a negative evaluation to something, my stance toward it changes—cautious at least, perhaps evening avoiding it. Certainly not wanting to endorse, engage, or support it. It would be a big deal—a huge loss for me at least—if I decided to view the world, my community, my neighborhood as a nasty situation in which survival was my primary objective.

If the entire subject seems a bit muddy to you, don't fret. A survey of religious responses to the world reveals a hung jury. Some work diligently to separate as much as possible. Some try to establish a playbook of how to take advantage of the good while avoiding the negative temptations that beckon. Others attempt to blend in, sort of like double agents who work both sides of the party. Sincere, well-intentioned folks have been divided on this matter for quite some time. No wonder it remains a divisive topic.

Even as I want to avoid a nasty assessment of the state of the world, I can wholeheartedly embrace the importance of encouragement as a key part of the faith experience. I recall a day during my service as a pastor when I realized the meeting I served was filled with individuals who spent their week motivated by their faith to make a positive contribution in the community. Not just on the sunny side of the street, either. Some of them rolled up their sleeves daily and dealt with heart-wrenching cases in social services, counseling, health care, and the like. Sundays at the meeting were times of renewal and encouragement, feeding their souls and recharging them to resume their good work the next week. However difficult their efforts were, I don't think I ever heard any of them speak of it as nastiness they were trying to survive. They used terms like hardship, brokenness, tragedy. Rather than a mentality of survival, they spoke of sharing light in the world or offering hope and healing to those who were hurting, suffering, or in need. They were working to transform rather than avoid. That is a huge difference.

Speaking of flats, a memorable one occurred years ago on a Sunday morning when I'd been invited to speak at a worship service about forty minutes from my home. Twenty minutes into the trip, the ride became uneven and bumpy. Sure enough, the front tire on the driver's side was flat. There I was on the side of a state highway in North Carolina in a three-piece suit, on my knees, putting on the spare. Several cars passed, but none stopped to offer help. Didn't a guy in a suit on a Sunday look like he had somewhere to be? I didn't need any help, but it sure would have been nice to have had some. I especially wanted to avoid arriving at my destination covered with grease and grime.

Wouldn't it have been ironic if I arrived late to the church, I thought to myself, and one of the attendees had passed me by on the road? It would have been easy to write my own "woe is me" version of the Good Samaritan parable where I was the one in the ditch, and countless ones ignored my need. From there, it would be an easy step to wail about people's insensitivity in this nasty world. More likely, everyone else had their own place to be. They weren't ignoring my need as much as they were focused on their own plans.

That line of thought doesn't require anyone to be a villain or mean-spirited. The life that unfolds before us and around us has complicated plots and trajectories, regarding most of which we're unaware. Better to make our peace with the fact that not every break goes our way, not everything revolves around us at the center, and not everything beyond our control is necessarily a threat to us. Nasty or otherwise, we face the task of choosing how we will proceed. Those choices are greatly influenced by how we've settled questions about how we view and relate to the world around us.

Two summers ago, I wound up with another flat, though this one was on my bicycle. The tire could not be repaired, and I was a few miles away from the trailhead where my car was parked. Faced with the prospect of a l-o-n-g walk pushing a bike, inspiration struck: I called an Uber. Often, a quick inventory of the resources at our disposal will open a new solution to life's flats in a way that doesn't reduce us to playing the victim or living perpetually on the defensive. We may never sort out the answers to all of life's questions. As long as we use inflatable tires, you can be assured we will never completely be rid of life's flats. That doesn't mean the road is bad or that errant nails had it in for us or that "they" were out to get us. Flats happen, but that doesn't have to ruin the trip.

Query for Contemplation: Our commitment to peace is enhanced by our inner state of being. As you pause and consider your view of your world and community, what images come to mind? Do you find optimism and reason to hope, or do you sense worry and despair? What effect is that reaction having on you?

Across the Valley

We pulled off the highway and stopped.

The driver turned off the engine. From our vantage point, we could look across the valley and see the outline of a city against the blue sky. "That is Jerusalem," our guide announced. "Some days, I bring my children to this very spot and park. I point to the building where their mother works. They want to know why we can't visit her there. How do I explain that to my kids?"

His name was Mustafa. He was our guide for the five days we visited areas governed by the Palestinian Authority. Mustafa was passionate and opinionated—and why wouldn't he be? Like so many others, his life has been turned upside down by the conflict in the land of his birth. He wasn't always a tour guide. In another life, he traveled to Jerusalem every day for a job in the field of finance, while his wife made a similar journey to work in the nursing profession. That changed sometime after the Oslo Accord. As he put it, Jerusalem needed nurses, so his wife was able to continue working at the hospital. The financial field didn't suffer from a lack of Israeli candidates, so he was fired. The person who took his position was less qualified. He merely lived on the right side of the wall and had the right connections. Now Mustafa's wife crosses the checkpoints every day into Jerusalem for work, while he and his children are not allowed to enter the area. Individuals who cross the border on foot have their documents checked. Differently colored license plates help regulate traffic flow. Cars and buses are searched frequently. It was an inconvenience for us while we were there; it must be a royal pain for those who endure that process daily.

Mustafa is a fine guide. He is patient and knowledgeable and is an effective educator. But it was clear that guiding is not his passion. He's a bit angry, and I can't blame him. Surprisingly, his frustration is directed at Israel and the Palestinian Authority alike. With the former he sees false claims, stolen land, and broken promises. He is convinced they play games with water, electricity, and transportation, all of which emphasize the inequity of the system. With the latter, he is appalled at the corruption among the elected leadership that has managed to prosper to indecent proportions while the people they represent suffer for survival. He gave the example of an official who had no wealth when elected but now has a net worth of ninety-six million and recently purchased his own private jet. He wants to know, how does this happen? And how can this leader be trusted to reform a system, even if broken, when it benefits him so much?

There is plenty to inspire marvel within the West Bank. Jericho holds the remains of a city and tower dating to 10,000 BCE. In Bethlehem, the Church of the Nativity connects travelers with the birth of Jesus. In Hebron, the Cave of the Patriarchs marks the spot where tradition says Abraham and Sarah, Isaac and Rebekah, and Jacob and Leah are buried. That site, in particular, brings visitors face to face with the divided world of Muslims and Jews. A mosque occupies part of the site; the other side houses a synagogue. Getting from one to the other requires passage through multiple checkpoints. With that, we step right into the reality that besets the population trying to make a home in this land that means so much to so many.

I feel for Mustafa and, for that matter, for the entire region. During my few days there, I had the opportunity to listen to Israelis, Palestinians, Jordanians, and Egyptians speak about the challenges of living in their region. In each case, I found myself thinking their point of view had a certain logical coherency built upon the blocks they chose to use—even though it was at odds with certain points of the others' positions.

If I gained nothing else from those conversations, I came away with a new appreciation of the complexity of the conflict. An Israeli living in a West Bank settlement began his story by noting that, in ancient times, the area was known as Judah, until the emperor Hadrian changed it to Syria-Palestina to spite the Jews after the Bar Kochba revolt. In this settler's perspective, no Palestinian people existed prior to 1948. This meant the Jews had the earlier claim to the land.

A Palestinian started his explanation by emphasizing the Canaanites and other groups who preceded the Jews in the area. Those people were their ancestors, and their prior claim to the land established their legitimacy.

One thing seems certain: this problem will not be fixed by a "deal." The rifts between them are significant. They deepen with each new trespass or injustice. This disagreement is about more than dollars and cents as an incentive to settle. It is about identity. It is about heritage. It is about justice. Beneath those encompassing issues, on a basic level, it is as simple as wanting the chance to live a life of relative peace and happiness. That is true for all involved. The numerous occasions where I met Palestinians and Israelis working cooperatively underscored that point.

War is a terrible habit humanity has developed as a means of solving disagreements. Righteous rhetoric used to justify the action often glosses over more ambitious and profit-driven motives. I've often thought the world would be a less violent place if, instead of engaging armies or dropping bombs, we could lock world leaders in a small room with boxing gloves, a chess set, or even a deck of cards. We could refuse to let them out until they settled their differences. Instead, those in power get to use ordinary citizens as pawns in their campaigns while they themselves stay safely out of harm's way. Hardly any of the people thrown into the battles waged to satisfy the egotistic greed of the powerful really wants to risk their lives or be responsible for snuffing out the lives of others. I am not saying that nothing is worth dying for, but I doubt that most of the world's conflicts rise to that level.

If only we could strip away the ulterior motives that drive so much of the world's drama. That may be a utopian dream, but it's worth pursuing. One sign caught our attention in Jordan: "Heritage belongs to humanity. Take care of it. Help us preserve it." We all have a stake in this world. But we're going to have to learn to share if we are to survive.

Query for contemplation: As you think about the circles in which you travel, are there places you wish to go but are prevented from doing so because of who you are? Are there moments when your attitudes and actions interfere with the efforts of others to pursue their own course? How might a commitment to the ideal of peacemaking influence those encounters?

Resistance Isn't Futile After All

There were literally thousands of them. Some towered several feet in the air. Others could have been carried in the hands of a small child. The area was crowded with crosses, with no particular order evident except to allow for footpaths through the space. Over a hundred thousand crosses stood on this hill, each one occupying a spot, each one representing a life, a story, a dream that someone wanted remembered. This was my impression of a recent visit to the Hill of Crosses.

The Hill of Crosses is a pilgrimage site located in Lithuania. The stories attached to each individual cross make it a special place for those who add their contribution to the site. Each cross represents a life that mattered to someone. Standing alongside so many others helps insure that it will not be forgotten, even as it loses part of its own individuality once it is placed among the group and becomes one among many. Creating a pilgrimage site was probably not on the minds of those who placed the first few crosses there. As I listened to the history of this place, it struck me as an act of witness and resistance. Witness to the loss of someone important and resistance against forces that sought to silence and eradicate a culture and a religion in the effort to occupy and dominate a territory.

One piece of information that weighed heavily on my heart even before encountering the hill was the fact that, for much of their history, and particularly most of the last two hundred years, up until the dissolving of the Soviet Union, Lithuanians were exiled, occupied, or ruled by someone else. That bit of history was already churning within me, causing me to wonder what it would be like to live under foreign occupation, have my land stripped away, and even have my citizenship revoked because my country was no longer recognized as a sovereign state. The plight of Indigenous people came to mind as an example of similar sorrowful experiences involving my homeland. I will admit to being grateful for being removed from these incidents directly, but they do add to a nagging question of, "Why is it that so many nations are not happy unless they are oppressing someone else for their own gain?" That is the kind of query that sobers the moment, but the story of the origin of the Hill of Crosses offers a bit of realistic inspiration.

Tradition says the first crosses appeared back in the 1830s, during an uprising against Russian oppression. Some people went off to fight in the rebellion, never to return. Others mysteriously disappeared, possibly kidnapped and removed from the area, leaving distraught family members to speculate about their fate. Within those uncertain times, as a new regime sought to squelch dissent and intimidate opposition, a few found a quiet way to commemorate their losses. They erected crosses on the hill to remember those who were missing.

The use of a Christian symbol for remembrance was, in itself, an act of resistance against a movement that sought to silence religious expression. During the mid-to-late twentieth century, under Soviet occupation, the hill became a more important site as a symbol of resistance as the Lithuanians sought to protect their heritage, religion, and identity against the efforts to create a more singular identity within the Soviet empire. Apparently, the hill's uniting power was a nuisance to the oppressors because they bulldozed the site three times; but each time, it returned. They reportedly planned to create a reservoir there so that the whole site would be underwater. Fortunately, that never happened.

Our visit to the Baltic capitals was filled with stories and images of resistance and survival. In the city of Vilnius, we stood on the plaza marked by a commemorative tile, identifying the ending point of a human chain that extended from there through Riga, Latvia, to Tallinn, Estonia. Two million people stretched almost 420 miles as a demonstration for independence. (Read more about it here: http://www.thebalticway.eu/en/history/.) Our guide shared with us her own experience of joy the day she was finally able to trade her Soviet-issued documents for a passport identifying her once again as a Lithuanian. A ninety-two-year-old woman described her living conditions the years she was taken from her home and exiled to a labor camp in Siberia until she convinced the driver of a supply truck to allow her to stow away in his vehicle as he exited the compound. We had lunch in the home of a family with a small fruit winemaking business that had managed to retain a portion of their property by burying the family silver and replacing curtains with burlap so that they were not judged to be among the elite. (To this day, later generations of the family have not discovered where exactly the silver is buried.)

This region is full of stories of witness and resilience. These days, I find those to be two admirable qualities. Witness because our lives cannot help but testify to the things we value. How nice it is when our living matches the things we say are important to us. The alignment of our life and our values is a key to faithfulness as well as to happiness. Resilience because it keeps hope alive in the face of opposition. In my travels, I have stood on the grounds where some of the worst atrocities heaped by one group upon another have occurred, learning of them in a way that simply reading a book cannot convey: the beaches of Normandy, mass grave sites in Cambodia, concentration camps in Poland, a genocide museum in Rwanda to name a few. Each of those places shows evidence of recovery and continuation, though not without costs and scars that document the pain. Humanity's capacity to inflict suffering on others is matched only by the resilience of the human spirit. Time and time again, hope persists among those who survive.

Like a dandelion pushing its way through a parking lot crack, resilience means we continue to be drawn toward and push to the light even in difficult circumstances.

I appreciate the stories of these Lithuanian friends and many others. They remind me that, sometimes, we only see the value of the life we enjoy when it comes under threat. That feels more important to me as I struggle to understand the divisiveness, globally and locally, that seems more volatile than ever before.

These stories demonstrate that witness is important if the life you value comes under siege and is not to be obliterated and forgotten.

And perhaps, most importantly, they remind me that, no matter how bleak the moment is, resistance is not futile after all. That is the sort of advice that is worth tucking away in a place where it is not easily forgotten.

Query for Contemplation: Where have you seen resilience prevail against harmful or oppressive ambitions? Where might a resistant effort by you be needed?

By the Zacchaeus Tree

"So now what, you want to kill me?" The question shouted by the Palestinian man startled me. I was caught completely off guard. Especially since he was asking me.

A few minutes earlier, our small group had filed off the bus near an old but still stately sycamore tree. We were in the West Bank. Having come from the ruins of ancient Jericho, we were now stopped at a tree reported to be the one a man named Zacchaeus climbed so that he could catch a glimpse of Jesus. Zacchaeus was a short, curious, and seemingly clever fellow who also happened to be a tax collector. If you are unfamiliar with the story, you can read it in Luke 19 in the Bible. Now known as the Zacchaeus tree, it is reportedly over two thousand years old. Could it be the actual sycamore mentioned in the story? "Who knows?" is the most honest answer for this and many sites throughout this area. It may or may not be the exact tree, but why not grab a photograph while remembering the story?

A fellow traveler was about to snap Judi's and my photo when a fistful of textiles were shoved into my field of vision, and I became aware that someone was shouting at me. The person attached to the hand asked if I wanted to buy a keffiyeh, the traditional Arab headdress. I was posed for the picture and eager to have it taken before someone else stepped into the frame to get their own shot. In that hurried state of mind, I did not even look at the person demanding my attention. Instead, I motioned for him to go away.

In response to my actions, the zealous salesman seized the moment and yelled, "Don't wave your arm at me. Don't treat me like that!"

Maybe it was the jet lag. Perhaps it was my truest, gut-level response to being yelled at by a stranger. Who knows? I shouted back, "Then don't stick your arm in my face when we're trying to take a photo."

Not to be outdone nor ready to concede, he barked, "Then you say, 'Excuse me, I am taking a photo. Could you please wait?'"

By then, I was fully engaged in this moment and countered with equal intensity, "Why? You did not have the courtesy to say, 'Excuse me, can I interrupt you and ruin your photo?' did you?"

Ordinarily, I would feel bad about raising my voice, but the man's next response floored me: "So what now, you want to kill me?"

I was stunned. Looking directly at him, I replied, "Of course not. How do you go from 'stay out of my photo' to my wanting to kill you? My wish is to enjoy this place and take this picture. That is what I want." He walked away.

After Judi and I took the desired photo, we observed the man pushing his wares whenever possible. I approached him and said, "I apologize if I seemed rude earlier. It was not my intention to offend you." He placed his hand on my shoulder, kissed my cheek, and tried to position the keffiyeh on my head.

"Here. This is for you," he said.

I answered, "Thank you, but I am not interested in buying it."

"No, no. It is a gift for you," he insisted.

Past experience had taught me that accepting the gift leads to a request for payment. Give something to be remembered by—or perhaps a few dollars. I had seen it before.

Encounters like these are simply a part of the travel experience. Anticipate it. Prepare for it, unless you want to bring home a suitcase full of unwanted items. Honestly, it is not completely out of line with what we regularly face. A harsh reality is that, at home or abroad, in a historic location or at the local market, to those with goods to sell, we are all potential customers. Failure to engage any who appear on their radar is a missed opportunity. Missed opportunities affect the bottom line, which impacts quality of life. That is true whether we are at the local farmers market, an international spice bazaar in an unfamiliar land, or standing in front of a two-thousand-year-old tree.

The rules of engagement vary from place to place. Think about it. When shopping at your local department store, no one from housewares will chase you around the store, hounding you to purchase an instant pot while you cruise the footwear section. A different set of etiquette is in play. (Though, come to think about it, Google ads chase me all over the internet.) However, at a basic level, the goals are similar: exchange something they have (product) for something they want (your money). That is the case whenever we set foot into someone's sales territory.

I can appreciate that reality and, for that reason, respect the man who tried to sell me his wares. He needs food daily and a roof over his head. Others may depend on him as well. All of us face the challenge of finding ways to acquire the resources we need to survive. Some are fortunate enough to have a skill or service that others will pay for. You may even find an organization that will hire and compensate you on a regular basis. Those who are not so lucky are forced to find other means to subsist, even if the activity is not one they relish. That is one reason I attempt to be polite to telemarketers. I despise their unsolicited phone calls, but that is their job. It may be the best opportunity they have to provide for themselves. (Of course, these days, robocalls have put most of the humans out of work, it seems.)

I doubt many of us want to view life as little more than a sequence of transactions where people and things are evaluated based on how they might be beneficial to us. We much prefer that deeper values ground us with altruistic motives, shaping our interactions with others. If that is the case, then behind the various methods utilized to secure a desired outcome exists a fundamentally important question: How shall we initiate and cultivate the engagement?

For instance, a salesperson wants to be noticed. Shall a passive or aggressive approach be utilized to achieve that goal? If the potential customer is not interested in your attention, then what do you do next?

My experience at the Zacchaeus tree prompted me to think seriously about that next step. Frequently, a concerted effort is made to escalate the situation. Keep the connection alive. Intensify the situation. Here is the thing: how one chooses to raise the stakes matters. This is a crucial moment in these encounters wherever they occur. Shouting can be one means of escalating an exchange. For me, questioning my intent to harm heightened the tension of that moment by the Zacchaeus tree. If actions trigger reactions, and rhetoric draws lines in the sand, we can quickly find ourselves overcome by our need to save face.

Next steps matter in our interpersonal exchanges. I will be unpacking many of the experiences from these travels for a while, I am sure. One thing that was clearly reinforced under the sycamore and numerous other times is that life is complicated, especially when we try to take the other's point of view seriously. Most of us are merely trying to make the best of what life has dealt us even as others think we are trying to take advantage of them. Easy solutions are difficult to come by. It would be simpler to throw up our hands and leave it at that, insisting that life's complexity justifies poor, manipulative behavior. But I prefer to live in the hope that we can do better to and better by one another. After reflection on the exchange with my keffiyeh-hawking friend, I find that a few questions have settled on the front burner of my mind when engaging others:

- Can I be forthright about my intentions?
- Can I articulate my true motives?
- Can I be considerate of another's preferences?
- Can I respect others' rights to be uninterested in what I am offering?

- Can I be gracious and tolerant, at least initially, when facing irritating tactics?
- Can I be kind in the face of rejection as well as when I am the one rejecting another's offer?

Taken together, these questions can be a tall order to fill, but I think it is worth the effort. When Jesus acknowledged Zacchaeus as the tax collector he was and still chose to dine with him in his home, it turned out be a transformational moment for Zacchaeus. Maybe that is possible for the rest of us as well. I have my own work to do in this regard.

Query for Contemplation: What stereotypes or biases do you see that disrupt and complicate relationships in your community? Are any of them dominant in your own thinking?

Toward a Testimony of Peace
Questions for Further Reflection

1. In living with others, what are ways that you can help eliminate the unnecessary conflict and especially the escalation of disagreements toward violence?
2. Can you identify particular hot button issues where you find it difficult to maintain composure conducive to maintaining a commitment to peace? What makes these topics so controversial? What steps can you take to defuse them?
3. Philosophically or theologically, is peace always the right commitment? Why or why not?
4. When you survey locations where violence repeatedly prevails, can you determine its root causes and imagine ways to restore wholeness?
5. As you face differences with others, how will you commit to actions that unite rather than divide?

Integrity

When Honesty Matters and Trustworthiness Is a Given

Care less about being perfect and more about being true to what matters. Integrity asks us to live an undivided life, manifesting consistency of character wherever we roam. When paired with kindness and truthfulness, integrity builds amazing levels of trust between parties of all sorts.

Fill My Cup

Ever have days when you feel like the class dunce? I do. Those occasions are slightly more embarrassing when they occur in public places where others have the opportunity to witness your brilliance. If you're fortunate, you'll be able to laugh at yourself and move on, though that is sometimes easier said than done.

For the past twelve months, my wife and I served as part-time interim co-pastors for a Friends meeting located near our home. Thanks to the pandemic, we had little else on our calendar, and it felt as though the Spirit was nudging us to say yes, which we did. With appropriate precautions, except for about an eight-week period beginning at Christmas, this small group met face-to-face throughout the year.

Every Sunday as I prepared for worship, I filled a small disposable cup from a bottled water dispenser located in the kitchen. The fact that bottled water was available, and this was rural Indiana where well water often has heavy iron content, led me to assume the tap was off limits for drinking. No one ever said as much, but why else would a water dispenser be available? This wouldn't be the first small church I'd seen with non-potable water. Plus, I never witnessed anyone filling a cup to drink at the kitchen sink. This became part of my Sunday routine. Each morning, I filled and took a cup of pure, refrigerated water from the dispenser. Not only was it refreshing, but it also had the added bonus of allowing me to discreetly lift my mask and liberate my face for a few seconds with each sip.

Over the course of a year, I watched the water line slowly drop in the five-gallon container. As we entered the month of June, I wondered which would expire first—the water supply or our contract. And by the way, what kind of refill schedule were we on that the machine hadn't been serviced in a year? Who oversees that detail? When a request was made for any additional agenda items at the end of the June business meeting, I dutifully and respectfully pointed out the water tank needed to be refilled and asked how that was ordinarily handled. Every face in the room immediately lit like light bulbs, complete with a light chuckle and a twinkle in their eyes. There was no water service. One of the members filled the bottle from the kitchen tap when necessary. Sometime in the past, they had used bottled water, but once a new softener was installed, that was no longer necessary. They kept the unit because the children enjoyed drinking from it. For a moment, I felt a little foolish, ready for the dunce hat and a seat on a stool in the corner, but it was good for a laugh among friends. The tank was magically refilled by next Sunday. When the time came to fill my cup, I went back to the water cooler, even though its contents were the same as the liquid available from the tap. Even young habits die hard, I suppose.

In an odd sort of way, this incident helped me feel closer to the group. Perhaps this was because I now knew one more innocent detail that revealed a sliver of their history and a slice of how they nurture their children. Or perhaps it was because I'd momentarily asked an innocent question and wasn't voted off the island. The experience even prompted a few thoughts about the value of integrity in social exchanges as well.

Sometimes things are exactly what they appear to be. The apparatus located in the kitchen was, indeed, a bottled water dispenser. It looked like one. It functioned like one. It was one. Even though it was what it appeared to be, it wasn't what it seemed to be. That is to say, the water wasn't purified. It hadn't been distilled. It wasn't collected from some glacial pool located in a remote, undefiled water source hidden somewhere in the French Alps. It was still good old Indiana well water. Even though it won't kill you, it might make you grimace were it not for the effect of the water softener. On those occasions when things aren't what they appear to be, we're often reliant upon the knowledge and kindness of others to share the needed information that allows us to better understand what is before us.

On this huge globe we call Earth with its billions of daily situations and transactions, such reliance multiplies significantly and becomes more crucial to our safety and success. Integrity is often missing from the equation, which complicates things immensely. As an example, last week, while in the supermarket, I was surprised to see that the sodium and sugar content of a popular breakfast cereal was lower than that of one purported to be healthier. I was about to put the healthier cereal back on the shelf, muttering about false advertisement, when I noticed the serving size on which those numbers were based. A serving of the sugary cereal was one third less than the other brand. Once adjusted for that detail, the picture looked different. Was the information on the box true? Yes, but in an effort to compete in the marketplace, it was reframed so that things weren't exactly as they appeared. Who knew that understanding the truth, the whole truth, and nothing but the truth, could be so tricky or that just the facts alone could mislead you if you failed to notice just one of them?

It reminded me of a conversation with a friend who is a partner in an investment firm. He left his very first job in the industry to start his own office when he realized that weekly sales competitions with bonuses for the winner meant that the company was enticing its employees to put their own gain ahead of their clients' interests. That created an uncomfortable ethical dilemma for him. The stock of the day was legitimate. It may or may not have been a good value at the time. Even if it was, it wasn't necessarily a good choice for everyone's portfolio; but in order to reach the sales goal or win the competition, those details needed to be ignored for the sake of a sale. His experience serves as a reminder that something can be legal and even encouraged but not ethical or moral. Integrity helps us begin to discern the difference and act accordingly.

For whatever reason, integrity is sometimes viewed as optional and nonessential in many social exchanges. The fact that not everyone embraces it as a worthy ideal is, itself, a topic worth exploring. Meanwhile, a fed-up public has good reason to be skeptical of processes that deceive or deprive, cheating the many and rewarding the few. When integrity is lacking, trust begins to erode. Just as a rusty-bottomed bucket won't hold water, neither will the excuses used to justify the actions. Politics, policing, lending practices, and health care costs, to name a few, garner the headlines and leave us wishing for a better day. Decisions made affect the quality of life for many. Are they made in our best interest? Are they free from efforts to game the system or unfairly benefit a privileged few? We understandably call for better performance and accountability from those in power.

This dilemma isn't limited to items in the news. Integrity or the lack thereof filters down to the simplest of exchanges between neighbors and friends as well. From property lines to play groups, integrity is the mortar that cements and stabilizes our relationships, helping ensure their dependability. Without it, an every-person-for-themselves mentality emerges, and in more extreme cases, a person can feel isolated or even preyed upon. Early Friends placed great emphasis on integrity as a cornerstone of their life together, perhaps because they recognized that reliable, trustworthy relationships transform a neighborhood into a community. Who better to tell you the truth about the water you drink?

As a standard, integrity can appear to be unattainable. When defined as "incorruptible," it may feel overwhelming because none of us is flawless. But taken as "undivided or honest," it is an idea that focuses on a commitment to be open and forthright, true to our principles. Integrity is less of a thing we do and more a way of being. Rooted among our most precious values, it infiltrates our philosophy of life and social exchange, insisting on an alignment between beliefs and practices. It becomes such a part of who we are that to try being otherwise creates a crisis of conscience.

Query for contemplation: What are some ways that integrity is present and demonstrated in your life? Can you identify moments when integrity is difficult to maintain?

Fake News!

Rest easy—this is not a political post, taking sides with one party or another. I am merely borrowing the term as a useful analogy. Stories, reports, facts, and figures presented as truth but branded by someone as false, designed to misconstrue, deflect, and mislead. Most of us are tired of this tactic, wishing people would simply take responsibility for their actions and commit to act and report with integrity.

Here is the thing that is often overlooked: fake news is hardly new. There are certain words or phrases, probably in every generation, that cause someone to lose credibility as soon as they are introduced into a discussion. Once unleashed, rational discourse around the topic becomes nearly impossible. "Communist" would be one of those terms from the 1950s and '60s. Spin a story about someone's communist affiliation, and their whole reputation was at risk, no matter whether the accusation was true.

As a North Carolinian, I find that the term "Southerner" has a lot of fake news attached to it. A Hoosier-born friend of mine remembers that, when he was in a doctoral program, he and some classmates were traveling to a conference in Virginia. One of them expressed shock that there could even be a doctoral program in the South because, of course, Southerners were intellectually inferior. Some still hold that opinion; I would call it fake news.

Labels that communicate stereotypes and prejudices are often founded upon fake news repeated and believed frequently enough that the assumptions become unquestioned. Even when they form unintentionally, it can take generations to overcome them. But there are also deliberate attempts to deceive and misinform. I think these are a bit more malicious because of the intent. On a recent trip to Mackinac Island, a historian provided an overview of the establishment and growth of the Grand Hotel, which is a centerpiece of the island's attraction. He shared advertisements seeking to recruit bookings in anticipation of the hotel's completed construction. The ads described the hotel as having more than a thousand luxurious rooms in a setting that sounded like paradise, while the actual plans only called for about three hundred rooms, and several of the amenities promised in the ads simply were not true. This was absolutely fake news, but it didn't matter. The goal was to convince, attract, and profit from potential clients, with no regard for the truthfulness of the claim. (And it worked!) That kind of advertisement was not limited to Mackinac. It was common practice in the business then; and some would say that is still true of the advertising world today.

In addition to stereotypes and misinformation, we could add another layer to the fake news collection: truth slanted to influence how one thinks about a topic. A movie review came across social media a few days ago. It read something like this: "It is the story of a young girl who came to an idyllic community where she killed the first person she encountered. The rest of the story documents how she and three friends eventually will kill again as she finds her way home."

Sound like a movie you know? It was posted as a review describing the *Wizard of Oz*. I think it was written in jest—it got a good chuckle from me, anyway—but that is not at all how I would describe that movie. At the same time, it is not untrue, is it? Dorothy's house lands on and kills one witch when she arrives. It ends with another witch melting as Dorothy makes her way home. More information reshapes how we hear and interpret the story, but the spin, the emphasis, the nuance, the overlooked details all contribute to how the story is heard.

I belong to a faith tradition that is concerned with knowing and presenting the truth. Admittedly, this is a dicey subject in an era where a competing claim insists there is no absolute truth, and what is true for you does not have to be true for me. That could make it arguable that no news is fake news if someone claims it is true. I don't embrace that point of view, but it does add complexity to the task of living together and trusting each other. In this milieu, I listen to the Christian sacred text as it offers admonishments and exhortations about the importance of avoiding incorrect teachings, inaccurate genealogies, false prophets, and the like. We are encouraged to discern between the spirits—to distinguish between what is true and what is not. It is basically a concern that one not be duped by fake news.

I presume that the preoccupation with avoiding fake news in the biblical texts is there, at least in part, because there were competing claims about what was to be believed and taught about God, Jesus, community practices, etc. Direction like that sounds simple enough. Beware of what is false; cling to what is true. As much as possible, ignore, if not end, the spreading of fake news. That would be a much simpler task if we could assume that those teaching, posting, and broadcasting a) were trustworthy, b) didn't have ulterior motives, and c) knew what they were talking about in the first place.

To be fair, some are trustworthy, don't have ulterior motives, are well informed about their subject matter but, like all of us, perhaps can't see their own biases or are missing one or two important pieces of information that significantly reframe the story. I recently read a book called *Factfulness*, the premise of which is that much of what we believe to be true about the world stands in stark contrast to the factual evidence. It seems that life and all the communication that goes within it can be really complicated, even in the best of situations. What is a person who simply wants reliable information to do?

Sadly, there are no quick fixes to such an age-old problem, but here are some potentially useful hints. First, be willing to wait to form an opinion. Today, we are much more geared to rush to a conclusion. If I have a question, I whip out my phone and Google it. Within seconds, I have an answer—well, a few thousand options actually, not all of which agree. The answer I find may be true, or it may be false, but I have a solution. I love technology, and you are not going to hear me bash its use, but I will say that the value of waiting is underappreciated. So, when we have questions, rather than rush to the easiest conclusion or explanation, in the spirit of many wise predecessors, take pause unless it is an urgent matter that cannot be postponed. The exhortation from Matthew 10:16 is generally sage advice: "Be cunning as serpents but gentle as doves." I take that to mean we should be wise, careful, gentle, and kind.

A second hint is as old as good reporting itself: "Know your sources." What was important in knowing who supplied the material for a printed news report that went through a vetting and verification process is exponentially more important in the age of digital overload where pressing "send" puts most anything in play as seemingly credible news. We too often fall prey to the "it must be true, I read it on the internet" mentality. Who informs or reports what you believe is true about God, about faithfulness, about current events from downtown bike paths to climate change to immigration? The complexity of life is only further confounded by the sinister motives that seem to occupy every waking moment of those who seek to sow seeds of disruption and sorrow.

Another hint: consult more than one source. After all, we have four gospels in the canon and a few others that were excluded. Why consult more than one? Because, when we proclaim a story—any story, really—we tell it in our language and from our point of view. Studies of oral tradition and storytellers have demonstrated that those always vary a little bit, even when we think they do not. By consulting multiple sources, we at least have the opportunity to see if and where there is a common core and a common agreement. We also have a chance to avoid living in an echo chamber where like-minded voices simply amplify and reinforce a position that may not be as straightforward as it is presented or as well-developed as it might be if it had the benefit of additional points of view.

Finally, know yourself. How do you most clearly hear and discern a way forward? This may be the most important of all. Quakers place great emphasis on the Inner Light, a metaphor for the Divine that suggests we have an interior guide who can teach and guide us. That suggests that one of the most important things we do as we contribute our part to this game of life is to recognize when, how, and what God speaks to us. Perhaps, it is the answer that rises in the quiet of the moment or what becomes obvious to you during the study of scripture or what breaks forth in your heart in the midst of fervent prayer or what strikes with clarity in the midst of corporate worship or what becomes convincingly clear in conversation with a trusted friend. There is a wealth of resources available to assist us as we make sense of the many layers of life and the often conflicting interpretations of it.

It seems we have always lived in an age where conflicting claims woo our allegiance. Apparently, it is part of what happens when many voices try to obtain success, assemble support, and influence their respective corners of the world. As if there were not already enough material out there, advising you on how to make sense of the world, I add this small contribution.

Query for Contemplation: In a world filled with voices that seek to persuade, are you mindful to know the sources that inform you, particularly if you have decided to trust them?

Not All Spam Is Created Equal

A late call roused her from her sleep, chasing away another sweet dream that would never be recovered. She hated it when that happened.

That was the price my friend paid when she volunteered to staff the food pantry. Sure, hours of operation were posted, but such signs to the hungry were what traffic lanes are to metropolitan motorists—mere suggestions. Somehow, word of who was staffing the pantry always leaked out to those who couldn't manage to take advantage of regular operating hours.

A persistent mother made her case for assistance. The volunteer responded that she was in luck, as the pantry would be open that weekend. Given her situation, the church would be able to help her. She should come on Saturday, and they would provide whatever aid they could. The volunteer was warm and kind, even though the late-night interruption tempted her to be more callous. Statistics played through her mind like a worn-out soundtrack, reinforcing the position that most transient calls are not legitimate, and many local calls are working the system. Still, she maintained her best demeanor of encouragement.

As my friend prepared to end the call, the mother's next words stopped her cold, "Ma'am, the opportunity this weekend sounds generous, but you don't understand. I need help now—tonight. My children haven't had a decent meal in two days. I can't wait until the weekend."

Somewhat begrudgingly, the volunteer agreed to meet the mother at the food pantry. It was either that or face a troubling conscience the rest of the evening. When she arrived at the doors of the pantry, a dirty but well-mannered young boy—maybe six years old—accompanied the mother. As the hungry pair watched, the volunteer filled one large grocery bag with food. She yawned in the process. She hated to admit it, but goodwill in this exchange was quickly disappearing. As the bag reached capacity, she heard the young boy exclaiming in a heavy whisper, "Mom–LOOK–we're getting SPAM!"

Well, his words melted the volunteer's heart. She had had her fill of SPAM as a child. SPAM loaf. Fried SPAM. SPAM and cheese. She had grown to hate it and had sworn she would never eat it again. Truthfully, she even hated to give it away simply because of her own negative associations. Never in a million years did she expect to hear it revered like a culinary delicacy. She was so moved by those five words that, in her words, "That family left with a car full of groceries that evening."

"Mom—LOOK—we're getting SPAM. Those aren't words I've heard very often, at least when used in a positive manner. These days, my issues with spam have to do with unsolicited electronic mail rather than unidentifiable processed meat, but I do remember having SPAM when I was a kid. I never knew exactly what I was eating or whether to be worried about the gelatinous goo that coated it. Once it had been fried for a few minutes, neither of those questions seemed to matter. It was not a favorite, but I did not mind eating it occasionally. Many people have strongly held opinions about SPAM; some may be surprised to know that, at certain points in history, SPAM has been hailed as an innovative meal option and has been received with thanksgiving.

One summer, while looking for things to see during a free day in Minnesota, I discovered an actual SPAM museum in the Austin area. If you think the meat used to make it is a mystery, try getting a straight answer on the meaning of the word SPAM itself. An impressive effort has gone into preserving the SPAM story, including photographing various celebrities attending SPAM public relation events there at the museum. Even for luncheon meat, I guess it pays to be seen with the right people.

Reportedly, the meat was a real lifesaver during World War II, as over a hundred million pounds were served to Allied troops. Even today, an estimated 12.8 cans are consumed each second. It may not make my weekly menu, but for some people, like the little guy at the food pantry, it rates as a delicacy.

Together, the food pantry and the museum trip create a useful reminder. Just because something does not suit my taste now does not mean others will not take great delight in it. If I have not traveled the road they walk, I probably will not fully appreciate their reaction to an opportunity that I may reject. Simply because I find something to be dated, questionable, or objectionable does not mean that it has never been appreciated or never occupied a worthy place in a different setting. I am reminded of that every time I take things to local thrift shops or browse through their shelves looking for the unusual, useful object that can be had for a bargain simply because it has been recycled. Those are basic, simple truths that we all should know, but they are easy to forget in the heat of the moment—or the middle of the night, as the case may be.

This reflection is not intended as an endorsement for or against the canned meat. It clearly played an important role in the 1940s and continues to rate highly with its fans. Rather, it is a reminder that there is usually more to a story than our own individual, limited perspective. We live with the tension of past and present, tradition and progress, good and evil, and the formidable challenge of navigating responsibly through life alongside a sea of others who are faced with similar challenges.

The risk with generalized statements is that they can be used to support things that really were always wrong or have outlived their usefulness. That perspective needs to be balanced with the equally bothersome risk of knee-jerk reactions and flash-mob responses to people and situations without taking time to get the full story or considering the source of what we see and hear. Everyone wants their truth to be heard and respected but finds it difficult to afford the same courtesy to others. Emotional rhetoric is powerful. Posted photos and videos are convincing, even though they never capture the entire story. Mob mentality is intoxicating, apparently. Once a rumor has been started or a lie has been spread, it is nearly impossible to repair the damage it causes.

These days, most of us face another kind of spam on a regular basis. Fake news and ulterior motives rank among the greatest nemeses of our current generation. They feed us a different kind of spam that is, itself, of questionable content and value. In simpler times, it was largely from bogus foreign contacts in grammatically suspect emails who promised boatloads of money once they had received our bank account information. These days, it shows up in our news feed or maybe even the six o'clock news—who knows anymore?

I embrace the reality of multiple perspectives and the value of laboring to understand the tastes of others. But I do tire of the duplicity and misdirection. I long for a commitment to integrity and the common good that makes possible those breakthrough moments where we see through another's eyes and are moved to help them, even though our own personal tastes have not changed. If you have developed a taste for spam (not to be confused with SPAM), be mindful that not all spam is created equal.

Query for Contemplation: If you are willing to live with an abundance of transparency for the sake of being better understood, how will you do so?

The Final Post

Social media has become such an ingrained feature of life for millions of people that a host of posts appears in our daily newsfeeds. Status updates sharing whereabouts, food choices, celebrations, frustrations, and a variety of commentaries are waiting each morning to help us start our day. Perhaps it is for that reason that, as I strolled through a cemetery recently, it occurred to me that, in a pre-social-media world, tombstones were like one's final post. Given one last opportunity to make a statement or suggest how one wants to be remembered, what would we say? I heard someone once quip that their epitaph should read, "See, I told you I was sick!"

You may wonder why I was strolling through a graveyard anyway. Thanks to my wife's diverse reading habits, I have become acquainted with a book titled *199 Cemeteries to See before You Die*. I do not expect to locate them all, but it did lead us to visit one of them, Graceland Cemetery, during a recent trip through Chicago. I must say, if you have to cross over to the other side and are looking for a paradisiacal setting where you can lay your remains, this one could make your short list. Who knew any place in the windy city could be that quiet and peaceful? With its mature trees, abundant lilacs, and tranquil lake, visitors may well wish they had packed a picnic lunch.

Graceland memorializes some significant pieces of Chicago history. People like George Pullman (think Pullman sleeping railway car), Potter Palmer (nineteenth-century real estate developer), Marshall Fields (founder of Marshall Fields department stores), and even Ernie Banks (of Chicago Cubs fame) are buried here. In many cases, it is inadequate to call these tombstones. Their markers are massive—monumental in effect. Palmer may take the prize for best view in the afterlife. His marker is a huge, Parthenonesque structure located on the banks of Lake Willowmere. Few of us get a lake view in life, let alone in death.

I intentionally use the word "monument" rather than "tombstone" to describe many of these markers. These are not simple stones with inscribed names and dates. They far exceed the usual custom of choosing one or two etched symbols like ivy or a decorative cross. It is the extreme opposite of an earlier Quaker practice of simple burial stones with an eighteen-inch height limit or even no marker at all. These monuments do more than indicate the location of the grave; at the very least, they give testimony to the wealth of the individual. I suppose their size and grandeur matches their prominence in life and seeks to preserve a memory of how their achievements helped advance society in their generation.

While I confess these mega markers seem a bit ostentatious to me, I cast no aspersions at them. They did, however, prompt me to wonder: if a tombstone is a bit like one's final post or status update, how would we choose to be remembered? In earlier times, certain symbols were frequently chosen—anchors (hope), clasped hands (unity or being received), boats (crossing to the other side), a dove (peace), and butterflies (metamorphosis). They represented things the deceased valued or hopes they carried with them. One creative stone resembled half of a house with the other part appearing to have been torn away—an apt representation of how death often leaves survivors feeling after losing a loved one. Some of these traditional symbols continue to be used, but these days, people often choose to blaze their own paths, representing their hobbies and passions—motorcycles or favorite trucks, for instance. Ernie Banks's marker is adorned with signs of his baseball career.

On occasion, those who mourn and reminisce decide how to remember the deceased. During a recent visit to Francis Bavier's grave in my hometown of Siler City, I was surprised to find several jars of pickles left at the base of her stone. Fans of *The Andy Griffith Show* may remember the episode where Aunt Bea's home-canned pickles tasted like kerosene, but no one had the heart to tell her. Aunt Bea may not have chosen to be remembered for her pickles, but that is how some fans pay tribute to her.

I wonder if the desire to be remembered is nearly universal. Why else would we create places of beauty to house our earthly remains and mark our places so that we can be found? Some would say that humanity has an innate desire to be immortal, with children and names on buildings being ways to make sure our memory survives our death. Yet it seems pretty certain that, unless we have been a mover or shaker in society, there is a good likelihood most of us will be forgotten within two or three generations unless tributes in public places keep our memories alive. Even knowing that will not likely deter us from trying to outwit oblivion.

So, when it comes time to make that final post, for those who come to pay an immediate tribute and for those who care enough to recall for years to come, how might you want to be remembered? The things worth remembering are seldom the fortunes one accumulates. Rather, it is the vision that motivated you—the philosophy that grounded you. It is the love you shared and the causes you fought for. It is the many ways you contributed to intersections of life where you met other people and made a difference in that moment. While impressive monuments can be artistic beauties, it is unlikely they rank near the top of the what-matters-most list. Rather, in the million moments between and beyond social media updates and the inevitable "final post" are the opportunities to create memories of deep significance. These are the things that will last as long as remembrance persists.

Queries for Contemplation: When you think of your life's journey, what are the things that matter most to you? Are those the things for which you are known now and will likely be remembered?

Toward a Testimony of Integrity
Questions for Further Reflection

1. When I identify the things that matter most to me, how do they reflect the priorities in my life?
2. When I consider where I contribute my time and resources, do they align with the things I say matter most?
3. What steps might I take to better bring my inner life and outer life into an agreeable alignment?
4. What kinds of situations most challenge my commitment to integrity?
5. When I think about the circles in which I live my life, what are some ways in which it is important that I speak truth and walk in truth?

Community

The Comfort of Companionship

Solitude can be a gift, whereas isolation can increase vulnerability. With togetherness, who knows what to expect? But when hospitality and respect abound, good things are always possible. They are essential seeds from which companionship can flourish and, with it, so also the gift of community.

Spiritual or Religious?

"I am spiritual but not religious." If I had a quarter for every time I have heard or read that phrase, I could finance my own church. The phrase is popular, trendy even—so much so that groups who study important cultural and religious issues have researched those who claim such an orientation. It does appear that a significant shift is underway with regard to religious life in America.

Initially, the phrase resonated with me. I was raised on a diet of Southern evangelical Quaker Christianity. It served me well enough in my youth, but I must confess to being exasperated with the institutional church from time to time. The first occasion of this occurred during a semester of church history in which I learned of the politics behind doctrinal decisions that were then promoted as truth fresh from the mouth of God. Perhaps that is the price of establishing orthodoxy. The Crusades added salt to the wound; I just have a difficult time imagining God authorizing religious wars. The frustration continues today as organized Christianity often puts more effort into self-preservation than into constructive leadership that addresses contemporary questions and great divides as people search to experience and know God.

Though the phrase "spiritual but not religious" may have initially resonated, I have since concluded that I have no desire to be counted among those ranks. For a while, I joked that I was going to start a new trend for those who were religious but not spiritual, but that route is fraught with its own perils. It tempts people to participate perfunctorily in rituals without being transformed by them as they contemplate their significance. I would not be happy with that either. (I suppose my Quaker leanings are showing here.) Instead, I advocate for being both spiritual and religious. Perhaps religiously spiritual or spiritually religious.

We really should not be surprised at the sentiment of "spiritual not religious." It is not a new leading-edge trend; it is a rather logical by-product in an era where there is large-scale rebellion against institutionalism and dominant narratives that overreach in their efforts to produce norms and encourage conformity. It leaves many of us in the proverbial baby-and-the-bathwater conundrum; dissatisfied with organized religion, this trend opts to empty the tub completely before refilling it.

This is an extension of the raging individualism that consumes so much of the current mindset. From "these rules do not apply to me" to loud smartphone audio blasting without earphones in public places, much of public engagement acts as if no one else is in the room, or if they are, they do not matter. Catchy phrases like "it takes a village to raise a child" or "think globally, buy locally" have good intentions but they seldom penetrate the core of our being to a point that individual sacrifice for the good of the whole replaces a focus on our personal agendas. It is much easier to affiliate with whatever reaffirms our personal preferences. Whoever coined the term "echo chamber" was spot on—by surrounding ourselves only with like minds, we reinforce our point of view.

It should also be noted that many who reject being religious have made that choice because of felt (and sometimes real) hostility and exclusion due to their political views, sexual orientation, economic class, etc. This, it seems, builds on the first two observations. The empowered individual and the questioning of dominant narratives encourage those previously silent to find their own voice. When those voices deviate too far from the norm (where is that invisible line located, anyway?), we may find ourselves faced with the choice to be quiet, fight for our place, or reject the system entirely. The rejection of religion but not spirituality may indicate an internal repositioning but not a complete abandonment of a religious connection. If that is what's behind the move, I can appreciate and applaud the effort. For all of their talk about love and acceptance, religions across the spectrum often demonstrate judgment and exclusion. Again, I find it difficult to believe that God advocates the ugliness that comes from that exclusion.

I have to confess, there are parts of this spiritual-but-not-religious perspective that do live and thrive within me. I insist on the freedom to define my own spiritual orientation and practices. In good Quaker form, I resist being directed by a centralized authority. And I attempt to exhibit generosity toward others who find truth and fulfillment in ways different from my own, including finding truth in other religions (admittedly, that has its challenging moments). Denominational affiliation and labels are not as important to me (and many of us) as they were to earlier generations. More than those badges of identity, I find good teaching and sincere fellowship to be of higher importance. When those are present, I am even open to accountability to certain norms and expectations. With that last statement, I realize that I value a little religion alongside my spirituality.

Why is that? It begins when I think about definitions of spirituality and religion. The word "spirituality" can sound mystical and deep, but my heart paid attention the day a peer described it as nothing more or less than "lived faith." Spirituality begins with inner connections where the Divine engages my whole being. It may be rich, heartwarming, or even unsettling; in every case, it serves to ground my being in ways that let me know I am part of an enormous movement of life. Those connections or conversations (or however one describes them) affect everything. From values to attitudes to actions, I am forever changed by those spiritual truths gleaned along the way. For that reason, the idea that spirituality must be lived, not merely a privately held idea, seems indisputable.

Religion, on the other hand, is often viewed as a cold system of rules that concentrates power in the hands of a few, taxes its participants, and imposes rules on its adherents, all while stripping the joy from life. There is no denying that it sometimes functions that way, but I do not think that is how religion is supposed to be. What passes as religion these days is the outcome of people living their spirituality collectively over time. What works once is repeated a few times. As several find a practice or a text valuable, they return to each other and to the practice. With time, their activities become regularized, even codified. Structures and authorities emerge. As repeated practice builds familiarity, the power and inspiration of the moment can fade. It seems even the best of spiritual practices lose some of their power in the transfer to the next generation who receives it as a given rather than experiencing it as fire. For that reason, religion can feel trivial. It is like wearing someone else's overcoat. It may keep you warm, but it doesn't feel quite right.

The part that is precious in the practice of religion is the community—the assembly of others who share a similar interest, passion, or commitment enrich the experiment. Together, we multiply the opportunities of internal support and external service.

A summer school experience illustrates this for me. It happened in my first course in biblical Hebrew at the divinity school where I was enrolled. I loved languages and could not wait to learn Hebrew. To my surprise, I was the only student enrolled. (I suppose there are more exciting ways to spend a summer.) The professor offered to teach me anyway. I jumped at the chance to have a private tutor. I learned the language well but must tell you that learning in a classroom of one brings its own challenges. I had to be well-prepared for every class, as there were no classmates to shoulder any of the load. Every question from the teacher was directed at me. Every incorrect answer came from me. There were no study groups to encourage me during the difficult stretches. No camaraderie or peer resources to enliven the journey. I am a guy who loves solitude and learning on my own, but I recall the weariness of undertaking this alone. No other experience has better illustrated to me the value of the corporate enterprise for certain things.

Spiritual practice is one of those things that benefits from a collective component. However precious and true my own spiritual experience is, I am one among billions. Even as I can name things that embarrass or disgust me within the practice of religion, there are many more that amaze me. The richness of the writings. The magnitude of service. The insights. The humility. These resources cannot adequately be replaced by YouTube videos (but what a great resource for everything from refrigerator repair to harmonica lessons).

My personal spiritual practice enthuses and shapes me. It is best fanned into flame by spending quiet moments alone, but as spirituality is lived, the communal connection found in organized religion is indispensable. It provides the opportunity to play with others. It presents a ready forum for the practice I need. My spirituality benefits from companions who help me see what I may otherwise not notice or affirm what I have come to hold as true or stand with me as we serve in difficult places. The onus is on those of us who participate in religion to guard intently against the hardening of the spiritual arteries as a consequence of routine and ritual.

Religion without spirituality may not be worth the bother, but spirituality without religion is difficult to sustain. I will not say it cannot be done, but I will say it is too important to risk. Thankful for the tension between the two, count me among the spiritually religious.

Query for Contemplation: What has been your experience of religion? How do you hold the tension between your individuality and your involvement with a religious community?

Lunch Anyone?

Living in a rural area where crowds are few and life's pace is slower has its advantages. It's the lifestyle I prefer, but there are tradeoffs. When you tire of listening to the corn grow or watching paint dry, finding entertainment options can be a challenge. Another sacrifice that comes with the territory is the sparse choice of upscale dining options, although we have our fair share of nearby fast food and chain restaurants. They give you a break from the kitchen but often leave you wondering why you left home in the first place. Wherever one lives, it takes effort to break out of the ruts that develop so easily in our routines. Many of us live with a lather, rinse, repeat mentality. Entertainment. Food. New experiences. Those are the sirens that summon me from the secluded area I call home. They are worthy goals, but they aren't always easy to come by in this neck of the woods.

With those goals in mind, a friend and I who meet regularly for lunch decided to venture off our well-worn path. We agreed to stay away from places we had been before. We would avoid chains. In no time, it became obvious that the next several months would be spent sampling the menus at the various dive bars in town. For those who wonder what that term means and to make sure we are all on the same page, dive bars are defined this way: "A well-worn, unglamorous bar, often serving a cheap, simple selection of drinks to a regular clientele." This is not an insulting definition, although it may be difficult to find glowing Yelp or Tripadvisor reviews for them. But there is more: "The term can describe anything from a comfortable-but-basic neighborhood pub to the nastiest swill-slinging hole."[2] To be clear, my friend and I have succeeded in visiting the well-worn, but to date have avoided any swill-slinging.

Simply making the decision to sample dive bars seemed like crossing a line or taking a dare. I was raised with a clear picture of places I should and should not frequent. In the Bible-belt South, staying away from establishments where booze was the primary beverage was drilled into young peoples' minds. Adults didn't necessarily follow their own advice, but that was the party line. Alcohol and carousing were apparently all that were necessary to grease the slippery slope toward the evil side from which all needed redemption. Religion can spend way too much time separating holy places from secular ones, then directing its own participants to play inside the approved areas. It's a point of view that fails to realize an omnipresent God can't be contained to designated areas. The fact is we may well find the Divine in the very places we have admonished others to avoid. In my formative years, dive bars were places that, if you dared go at all, you hoped no one saw you there for fear that it may tarnish your reputation. Maturity and retirement, not to mention a revised theology, can erase those types of concerns. So across that line we stepped.

Visiting these dive bars has been a positive experience for several reasons. For starters, it is too easy to visit the same handful of eateries when there are lots of local establishments that could use a little support. I remember a local smorgasbord where people would stand in line for hours during its heyday while, two blocks down the street, immediate seating was available at a locally owned gourmet restaurant. The latter lived a short life due to lack of business for reasons I never understood. Second, we've had some decent local, Midwestern food in these joints. Granted, some of it is nothing to write home about, but I have

---

2 https://www.urbandictionary.com/define.php?term=Dive%20bar (Accessed 8/29/2020).

had some pretty good breaded tenderloin sandwiches and a surprisingly good reuben. Most of the cheeseburgers only earn a ribbon if we're playing by the everyone-gets-a-ribbon-for-participating rules. (I've never been a fan of those.) Happily, none of them have made me ill. Thirdly, I have met really welcoming servers, who, while perhaps surprised by our presence, made us feel right at home just the same. My friend and I were able to enjoy just what we were looking for—a comfortable space, usually with minimal noise and distraction, where we could relax into the kind of rejuvenating conversation that is good for the soul.

Sometimes, everyone at the bar turns to stare when you walk in because, well, it's obvious you're not one of the regulars. I thought that only happened when visiting a new church. It does suggest that a sense of familiarity or perhaps even community develops in these places. However well-worn the place may be, its tracks have been ground out by those who experience a sense of belonging there. Sort of like the *Cheers* sitcom theme—sometimes you want to go to a place where everybody knows your name. Whether to sit and sulk or chat up the place, it's somewhere to come as you are and know that that is good enough.

The search for entertainment, new experiences, and food are worthy goals, especially when undertaken with mighty fine friends. But life is not always light-hearted. We need spaces where we can sit with unsung stories until they are ready to be heard. We can all use a place where, when we're ready to sing, there is someone willing to listen, however off-key we may be. How better to pass that time than with those we consider to be mighty fine friends. Particularly once we know that, wherever the joint may be, we can expect God to be present any old place where two or three gather together.

Whatever questionable moments I may have had during these dive-bar adventures, it was good to get out of the usual routine and see parts of town not on my ordinary route. You know you have survived a questionable choice when, as you exit, they assure you on the way out that you're welcome to come back any time. That may well be the badge of honor. To enter a place as a stranger and leave with a standing invitation to return anytime.

Query for Contemplation: Where might you occasionally venture off the well-traveled path in hopes of widening your base of community connections? What adjustments might you need to make in order to do so?

The Spaces Where We Gather

I cannot recall visiting any city in Central America that does not have a central plaza at its hub. Often occupying an entire city block, these plazas are usually lush with trees, ample shade, benches, and a decorative fountain. It is the kind of setting that invites a person to linger, and so they do. People of all ages gather, especially in the evenings. Elders play games. Youngsters race and dance. Teenagers test young love. Vendors populate the sidewalks, taking advantage of the foot traffic and ambiance. However difficult the day has been and however dangerous the city is by reputation or in truth, people gather. They relax, and the whole area hums with the exuberant energy of life. I love to park myself on a bench and watch the gamut of emotions expressed as life transpires.

There were not any "no loitering" signs posted. Law enforcement, while often present, did not herd the people along or insist they take their conversation elsewhere. This was spaced designed to welcome and hold its visitors so that community could be built. It is a piece of Central American life that I have often wished could be nurtured in places I have lived. That setting surfaced in my mind this week as I reflected on words from the prophet Zechariah: "This is what the Lord Almighty says, 'Once again men and women of ripe old age will sit in the streets of Jerusalem, each of them with cane in hand because of their age. The city streets will be filled with boys and girls playing there'" (Zechariah 8:4-5).

I had to wonder, what would be required for those words to be actualized? I think it would imply that an ethos of peace and tranquility prevailed enough that people had the opportunity to grow old rather than be mowed down by violence and recklessness in the prime of their lives. And having reached that ripe age where mobility was in decline, they still felt safe enough to toddle down the street to a favorite bench or coffee shop, meet their friends, and visit for a spell. It would mean that children's joy had not been snuffed out by abuse or fear, and their nearly inextinguishable light could animate a neighborhood. Given the chance, they would play for hours with their friends, not returning home until called for dinner; and parents would have enough confidence in their children's safety that they need not worry or fret about the decision to allow them to play outside of their supervision.

That description is not far removed from the world I knew as a child. While being Southern and rural has its own stigma in some circles, I recognize the privileges it held for me: peace, relative safety, a trustworthy community. Many, many places have rarely known that kind of stability, whereas I grew up thinking that was how life should be. I still see glimpses of it here and there, but I hear and read that it is missing in too many places.

I don't know if the world is actually more disrupted these days or if we simply know more about it thanks to social media and the twenty-four-hour news cycle. In either case, I am more aware of the chaos than before. Even the small town near me had an active shooter incident in one of its schools recently. In addition to the tragedy of that event, I watched parents' anxiety escalate as they sent their children off to school the next day, now knowing that they were not immune from random acts of violence.

The Zechariah passage I referenced earlier wraps its vision of the tranquil community within a larger expectation of restoration. Within that description, society's role was spelled out simply: "'These are the things you are to do. Speak the truth to each other, and render true and sound judgment in your courts; do not plot evil against each other, and do not love to swear falsely. I hate all this,' declares the Lord" (Zechariah 8:16-17).

There, it seems to me, is one of the rubs—a huge obstacle working against the possibility of relaxed elders and playful children. Somehow, much of our society acts as though deception, intimidation, and exploitation are the pillars of negotiation; truth is optional so long as your spin on the story is convincing. This is not limited to a few misguided individuals; it has somehow settled into the very systems and structures designed to support and sustain us. It is visible in some international negotiations. It is not uncommon in local politics. It rears its head in cutthroat business practices. It even influences the way neighbors and families approach their disagreements. Leverage, power, and greed are permitted to provide advantage to some—which means others are simultaneously disadvantaged and will eventually look for ways to rectify that situation.

Perhaps it has always been that way. When the dominant narrative of many inspiring success stories is peeled away, one finds a less flattering thread or two. Moving away from this ingrained tendency requires intention to live a different set of values and a commitment to consider more than one's personal gain. On occasion, I have tested a different approach to see what might prevail.

For reasons unknown to me, I enjoy handwoven carpets. This fascination began after seeing a presentation in Turkey that explained the process and the extraordinary handiwork required. Introductions to some of the workers plus conversations about working conditions and child labor were important parts of the visit; as you might imagine, exploitation is commonplace in some of these industries, and I had no desire to support such practices.

A few years later, a tour in Morocco included a stop at a local carpet shop where, after the usual presentation and hot beverage, I ambled around the shop, admiring the patterns and colors while waiting for the tour guide's call to the bus. But no one browses alone in these shops—at least not for long. Soon, a salesperson approached, and the banter began.

"You have an excellent eye." Flattery. "This is a fine selection," he said.

"Yes, it is nice, but I am not really in the market for a new carpet," I answered.

"My best customers are those who insist they are not looking for one. Make me an offer," he suggested.

"I really can't," I answered. "I have no idea of the cost of materials, of the hours of labor required, of the overhead costs. I haven't a clue as to what a reasonable price would be. I wouldn't know where to begin."

He insisted, "Just make me an offer. I am sure we can find an acceptable price."

"No doubt we could, but how would I know if it is a fair price?" I responded.

"Trust me. I will give you a good deal," he promised.

We played through a few rounds of this kind of conversation. After a point I said, "Look. Here's the thing. I don't have the information I need to make an informed offer. What I want is the cheapest price I can get that is also a just price for you. I have no desire for you to lose money on this deal because you need to earn a living, but neither do I want to be taken advantage of due to my ignorance. If you really want to sell me this carpet, here is what I would be willing to do. I want your absolute best, just price. My religious tradition has a long commitment to set prices and economic integrity. So you get one chance to price this carpet for me. You tell me the lowest price you are willing to take that is also fair to you. I promise you, I will respect your judgment. I will either accept the price or reject it, but I will not counter with a lower offer. If the price is one that feels comfortable to me, given that I don't know what this carpet is worth, I'll take it. If it seems too high for my budget, we will go our separate ways."

The salesman looked at me as though I came from another world. (Perhaps, in some ways, I do.) He thought about my request for a few moments and named a single price that suited my conscience. I enjoy this carpet every day when I sit in my living room. About once a year, I receive a phone call from Ibrahim or one of his associates who tells me he is in the US selling carpets at one venue or another and wonders if he could come by my home to show me his collection.

I have valued that experience with Ibrahim almost as much as the carpet itself. I still do not know if I received a fair deal. I do know it cost less than others were paying for similar carpets that day and less than I have paid for carpets in previous barter situations. More importantly for me, this was an opportunity to challenge a traditional model in which a legitimate need to make a sale is often corrupted by additional layers of deception and pressure—a manner of engaging others that I find difficult to justify.

Admittedly, this was one small conversation, but I like to believe that this kind of effort to recast our interactions with others has much to offer our attempts to live together in this small world. When we can meet the other with honesty and fairness, we may be able to revise the ground rules of our exchanges. Encouraging a move away from seeing our engagement as a transaction from which we alone should profit toward a relationship that promotes mutual value and respect for each one involved represents a seismic shift. It lays the kind of foundation that can nurture positive, ongoing relationships and draws people to form their own central plazas.

I do not suppose I will see a literal central plaza spring up in the little Midwestern village near where I live. But perhaps we could work on discovering other ways to create ample areas where playful children, wise elders, and welcoming spaces indicate we have together created a mutually respectful community.

Query for Contemplation: What are the gathering places that welcome and enliven you? What do you contribute to the quality of life that they offer?

And Then There Was Cake

Another birthday came and went in recent weeks. Although I've seen quite a few by this point, I am grateful for each one and enjoy a simple marking of the occasion. My wife, Judi, always bakes the cake of my choice as part of these celebrations. My request usually alternates between strawberry shortcake (the way my mother made it, of course) and chocolate cake with chocolate icing or perhaps a pecan pie, just to be different. We've been eating out less since this COVID business started, and because of that, Judi had already served up one of each of those sweet treats in recent weeks. I'd gladly receive a second one of any of them, but it seemed like the occasion called for something new.

I flipped through the cake section of her recipe box. It is filled with choices from at least three generations of ancestors, several cookbooks, plus a few internet recommendations. My eyes fell upon an index card with details for a peanut butter cake with peanut butter icing. Already a fan of peanut butter milkshakes, peanut butter ice cream, and peanut butter pie, I considered the discovery a portent from above and chose it for this year's celebration.

Judi later informed me the recipe claimed to serve sixteen people. I replied that they probably had very small people in mind or at least ones with dainty appetites, so not to worry about it. I rarely see more cake than anticipated as a problem, though it did cause a flashback to plans for our wedding reception thirty plus years ago.

I have a history with selecting overly generous cake sizes. To accommodate interested parties in our respective home states of North Carolina and Indiana, we had two marriage ceremonies when we tied the knot—which of course meant two receptions. Which of course meant two cakes. Judi did the bulk of the planning, and I was just fine with that so long as I knew where to show up and when to say, "I do." However, for the North Carolina reception, she wanted me to select the cake.

A local bakery provided a book with photos and descriptions of cakes, which I studied carefully. I chose what, in the photo, looked to be a modest-sized, three-tiered cake, accompanied by surrounding smaller, heart-shaped cake islands. I found it to be visually appealing and was quite pleased with my contribution to the planning. Sort of like instant replay with a basketball game, upon further review, my call was overturned when it became known that the cake served a few hundred guests—far more than we were inviting. I, of course, saw that as an opportunity for multiple slices for guests or for freezing and then having monthly anniversary celebrations as long as the supply lasted. Alas, we changed cakes instead. Oddly enough, as well as I remember the cake I chose, I can't describe the one that replaced it. All that is to say, I have a history of innocently choosing cakes that are larger than needed.

The peanut butter cake selected for my birthday was divine. I have savored every bite and moaned through most of them. There are a few slices still hanging out in the fridge, waiting their turn. One day, Judi asked if I wanted to invite a couple over and serve them cake. "Why?" I asked. She replied, "I just thought it would be nice to do." I answered, "It would be. I'm fine having them over, but why do you want to serve them my cake?" She left the decision up to me. Somewhat sheepishly, I must confess that I chose having more cake for myself.

Sharing is a funny thing. I'll share many things I have, especially once I am aware of a need. I am often a give-you-the-shirt-off-my-back kind of guy, but I hate it when someone else tries to force me to do it. I don't know how it is for you, but I notice an interesting internal tug-of-war where forced sharing begins to feel like being robbed even though the exchange is mostly the same as what I might choose to do if it had been my idea from the outset.

I have been thinking about sharing in recent weeks, though less about cake and more about space. There are similar dynamics involved. Living in a wooded area as I do, I expect a fair amount of wildlife to be around our house. It adds to the charm of the place, and I try to do them no harm. There are limits, though, such as if their activity damages our home. Last year, the trees were full of squirrels; this year, fewer squirrels are in the area, whereas the woods are abundant with raccoons.

Earlier in the spring, I watched a mother raccoon parade past the front of our house with five babies in tow. I'd hoped they were just passing through on their way to some luxury destination, but apparently, our place is their promised land. Now I have adolescent marauders trying to find a way to climb a birdfeeder pole so they can feast on the sunflower seeds we put out for our winged guests.

The fact that they are just doing what raccoons naturally do complicates the matter on a moral level. We all need to eat, and many of us return to eateries that satisfied us the last time we ate there. Should I work to thwart something that is merely acting according to natural instincts, even if it is taking advantage of generosity intended for others? The easiest solution would be to stop feeding the birds altogether, but should they be deprived of a food source for this reason? If I make my peace with sharing with the raccoons, but their activity destroys the feeder for yet a third time, do I still share without complaint? Alternatively, is the answer to trap and relocate the animals?

Where are my concerns about boundaries and property legitimate, and how do they interact with a live-and-let-live philosophy? Can I insist on my own freedom if it interferes with another's? What are the ground rules for working through the impasse that can quickly develop in those cases?

As superfluous as birthday cake and birdseed may seem in today's complicated world, some of these same dynamics are alive within most headline disagreements that rattle our communities. Islands and sea passage in the South China Sea come to mind, for instance. Unfair treatment of those whose skin color differs from our own provides an array of heartbreaking stories. These types of dynamics motivate and entangle most any activist cause, protestors and counter-protestors alike.

We all have ideas about what we want, need, and deserve, and we design plans to obtain them if possible. In the quest to satisfy those urges, it must be getting easier to not notice, not look, or not care how others fit into the equation. Why limit ourselves or share with others when we can demonize the other and justify keeping it all for ourselves? I can give you a dozen reasons why that is the wrong approach, but I also know it is not always easy to share space with others. Even if we agree with the psalmist that "the earth is the Lord's and all that is in it" (Psalm 24:1), some of us are pretty darned sure we are its appointed guardians, if not wardens.

Wouldn't it be great if sharing were a piece of cake? I guess I have work to do. Do you?

Query for Contemplation: Are there moments in life when you are possessive of things to which you feel justified in laying claim, even if it negatively affects others? Can you discern patterns or commonalities in those moments that merit attention?

Toward a Testimony of Community
Questions for Further Reflection

1. When thinking of the quality of community you desire, what are its most appealing characteristics?
2. What is your responsibility to help create a sense of welcome and hospitality among the company you keep?
3. What activities promote the level of engagement you need to feel integrated and rooted within a group?
4. How do you approach those whose differences from you are obvious, especially if they could be perceived as threatening?
5. How are various gifts and perspectives valued among the group so that all have an opportunity to contribute to the life of the group?

Equality

Looking for Worth in All the Right Places

Rooted in the idea that God does not have favorites, the testimony of equality begins by avoiding hierarchies and meaningless valuations that privilege some more than others. It eventually calls us to challenge the injustice and inequity we see around us, including that which is within us.

Sometimes You Are the Novelty in the Room

If I never have the opportunity to travel abroad again, I'll have no reason to complain. My wife and I developed a travel bug early in our marriage and have seen quite a bit of the world. We joked at the time that we'd travel while we were young and browse through photo albums when we were old and less interested in long plane flights and crowded places. I am not ready to declare myself old just yet, but I have been flipping through my pictures of late. Viewing them reminded me of how often I seemed to be a novelty to people we met around the world. Those who know me may not be surprised, arguing only to change the adjective from "novelty" to "oddity." You're entitled to your opinion. Heck, you may be right!

On a visit to southern India from a couple years ago, the people we met and the culture we experienced were the highlights of that trip. Much of it was brought alive by an exceptional guide who assumed everyone we met was happy to stop what they were doing and converse with our small group. To that end, he saw an opportunity when we passed a flatbed truck as we barreled down a highway toward our next destination. The back of the truck was stuffed with people, young and old, plus one goat! Together, they calmly bounced down the highway.

Our guide knew immediately that they were likely traveling to a local shrine where they'd sacrifice the animal as a thanksgiving offering. "We must talk with them," he insisted. So the driver of our bus sped ahead, outpacing the truck. A bit further up the road, we stopped the bus on the shoulder of the highway, where our guide exited the vehicle and flagged them down.

Our guide was correct. The group was happy to briefly interrupt their trip to tell us where they were going and why. According to them, their prayers had been answered. The desired blessing of a new child had come to fruition in their lives. They were going now to offer this animal in thanksgiving.

They wanted a photo (as did I). Maybe it was because I'm not Indian. Or perhaps they just like to meet new people. As much as they were offering a new experience to us, we, too, gave them one as well. That is a fact easy to overlook if we think our point of view is the only one alive in a moment of exchange with another person. I love the photo from that encounter precisely because I don't know any of the other people in it, but I had been momentarily welcomed and embraced.

We met through an act of serendipity, had a pleasant exchange, will probably never see each other again, but we all wanted to remember the moment anyway. The snapshot reminds me that a generosity of spirit can be found among strangers. It is a spirit that welcomes and invites us to sample one another's world. I find that encouraging in the midst of news stories filled with confrontation and violence between strangers who are certain their differences divide them. Even if we prefer our own ways, the encounter can build understanding, appreciation, and respect for the rich varieties in life—qualities that promote harmonious coexistence.

Another photo reminded me of the time I visited Tiananmen Square in Beijing, China. As I stood there, soaking it in, I was trying to imagine the protests that occurred in that very place. I was recalling that a first cousin on my mother's side had actually been there in those days, out among the people as the protests occurred, hoping that an

American observer might encourage restraint. That was the moment I was having when a young Chinese boy approached and asked if he could take a picture of me—something to remember the large, tallish white guy.

As it turns out, the photo was being requested on behalf of his father, who wanted a picture of himself photographed beside me. I gladly obliged. We stood together smiling, his head barely reaching my shoulder. Afterward he asked if he could touch my beard. That really caught me off guard, but why not? It was an odd moment to stand where these protests took place, feeling the sensation of a stranger's fingers running through my beard. In the midst of the novelty, we were both having a cross-cultural experience.

Then there was the time a Japanese tourist mistook me for a Greek fisherman and wanted to pose for a photo. Admittedly, we were on a dock in Greece. Wearing a Greek fisherman's hat and a yellow rain jacket, I bore a slight resemblance to Popeye's nemesis, Brutus, and looked the part, I suppose. My attempts to explain led to smiles, nods, and repeated requests for permission to take a photo. I finally resigned myself to play the part. He took the picture of us standing together with huge smiles. Now I'm probably stuffed in a vacation album tucked away in a Tokyo closet or maybe framed and hanging on a wall somewhere in a Japanese home.

We can probably all recall moments when we experienced something novel. It captured our attention and raised our curiosity. We experienced wonder, illumination, or maybe something less significant but nonetheless insightful and valuable. Those occasions are priceless in our understanding of the world in all its beauty and tragedy. They develop our perspective and deepen our ability to know and navigate. But here is the thing. There are moments—probably more than we recognize—when we are someone else's novelty. Their experience of us plants a memory deep within their heart where it is carried until, one day, something calls it forth again.

I was walking down a street in Antigua, Guatemala, a decade after my first visit to that city. Judi and I were recalling landmarks when a motorcycle pulled up beside us and turned off the engine. The driver removed his helmet and said, "Hola, Jay. Bienvenido de nuevo a Antigua." It was Henry, my Spanish instructor during my first trip there. I was blown away that he remembered me at all, let alone that he could recognize me on a sidewalk as he passed by. I knew that first visit had been a novel moment for me, but I had no idea it would be memorable for a teacher who sees several short-term students over the course of a year.

It is good to experience moments when you are the one different in a crowd.

Moments like these remind me that, at times, I am some else's novelty. While that can be surprising or even unsettling, it is often best to just relax, breathe, and go with the moment. Whenever we are the novelty in the room, we have the opportunity to help widen someone else's experience, expand their point of view, broaden their horizon, or stretch their boundaries just a bit. I would contend that those novel moments have made me a better person, more capable of enjoying life and making useful contributions to those I meet along the way. I only hope my novelty has done the same for them.

Query for Contemplation: When you find yourself in a novel situation, what instincts guide you forward? Do you need to feel that you operate from a position of strength or superiority, or can you receive them as people also made in God's image?

The Blessing of Corn

This has been the year of corn at our house. Vegetable gardening is a favorite summer activity of mine. After several years where one complication or another prevented growing a good sweet corn crop, that streak ended this summer. Judi and I have enjoyed fresh corn on the cob. We have frozen corn for use later in the year. We have included it in homemade vegetable soup, canned for the winter months. We have actually given more corn away to friends and neighbors than we have used for ourselves. A few days ago, I returned from the garden with 263 ears of corn in tow. That was for one day of what has been about a two-week, eight hundred ears and counting, corn apocalypse! Most days, even with the sweat bees swarming, I have been almost giddy at the bounty, enjoying the opportunity to share almost as much as consuming and preserving. For once, I have not even minded that a few deer and raccoons have feasted off our bounty. This whole experience has been a blessing.

    The concept of blessing is one of those topics on my short list of puzzles to ponder, and it came to mind several times during this harvest. I do not really expect to resolve the questions attached to these puzzles, but from time to time, I revisit them to think through the assumptions and beliefs attached to them. Picking and shucking corn allows ample time for reflection. I have long been fascinated with the theme of blessing. It first emerged in grad school, where I studied the concept of blessing as it developed in the Bible. Firmly planted in the creation story in chapter one, the theme strongly influences the rest of Genesis and becomes one of the measuring sticks used to determine faithfulness in later books. My book *Thanking and Blessing* considers the value of a spirituality of gratitude. I much prefer a vision of God and creation where love and goodness contribute to blessing rather than one where judgment and division lead to hatred and chaos. Even so, blessing remains on my puzzle list, and here are some the reasons why.

It is popular to say "I am blessed" or "I feel blessed." Those assessments generally reflect our sentiment that positive things are occurring for us, often interpreted as signs of divine favor. Numerous songs develop the theme that God blesses those whom God loves. Locate an old hymnal and hum along with "Count Your Blessings" or "Showers of Blessings." They were staples in the church of my childhood, and I continue to be fond of them. Search YouTube, and you will find more songs than you have time to play. "God's Got a Blessing with My Name on It" or "Blessing on Blessing" are examples.

The Bible's portrayal of blessing, both material and spiritual, as signs of God's favor is deeply planted in our tradition. The point is that we have lots of encouragement to view good things happening to us as gifts from the Divine. It is a perspective that has resonated with generations and shows no sign of abating. For the record, I have no desire to discount or dismiss the value or the importance of that theme. I do, however, wonder if we become careless in the way we use the term. Once we assign responsibility for the perceived blessing to God, it is beyond critique or question. It insulates our assumptions against challenge, even if they are fraught with inaccuracies. It justifies the situation, even in the midst of suffering or injustices that might result from what we identify as a blessing.

Recently I viewed a video clip in which the speaker described how and why her school attempted to teach students about gratitude. I am a huge fan of taking the idea of gratitude seriously. It voices appreciation toward others who have contributed to our good experiences. The affirmation provided encourages the other and nurtures positive relations with them. Gratitude acknowledges that we alone are not solely responsible for our happiness and well-being. It helps us begin to see the way our lives are filled with blessings alongside the various trials and tribulations we encounter. Frankly, I think gratitude is transformational. Even so, the video clip gave me pause. The speaker acknowledged that her life was blessed. I don't doubt the truthfulness of her experience, but as she listed the things she considered blessings, I found myself interpreting the sense of her words to really or at least equally mean, "I am so privileged."

Funny how word meanings and usage can change over time. There was a day when the term privilege suggested "honor." I am privileged to serve; I am privileged to introduce; I am privileged to accept—but these days, in some circles I travel, privilege is all about unearned advantage. Often the conversation connects with race, gender, or class. It is an important and difficult topic, and it strikes me as worth the effort to ask whether the things we may initially attribute to God's favor might in fact be more complicated than that.

The video was useful because it encouraged me to think about if and how blessing and privilege are at odds with one another. Consider this year's sweet corn experience. After years of no corn, this abundance easily seems like a blessing. It is, but is it due to divine favor or something else?

In the sense that one thinks all good things come from God, surely it is. But did God single me out for this abundance this year? Maybe not, but still, what a blessing to have it, right? Perhaps it is less a matter of being singled out and more one of adequate warmth, plenty of sun, rain at the right times, and good soil—all forces beyond my control that came together to create a corn-ucopian extravaganza.

I have long acknowledged that most of what makes a successful garden has little to do with me. I am mainly just the hired help, the gopher who goes for the seeds and battles the weeds and so forth. The wonders of germination, photosynthesis, and pollination are way beyond my pay grade. Still, I feel invested as a part of the process and blessed when it goes well. I might even pat myself on the back for my labor, feel a sense of pride in my garden, and thereby give myself a little credit. It allows me to think that, perhaps, I earned a bit of that blessing, accidentally buying into the idea that God helps those who help themselves.

But thinking a little further, some of that breaks down. Gardening is second nature to me because of how I was raised. Not everyone has that advantage. Land is required. I own land that I purchased over time out of the proceeds of my earnings. Not everyone owns land nor has the income to purchase it nor could qualify for a loan. And then there is the fact that this incredible looking corn was made possible because a friend shared his seed corn with me. Those who have no friends with access to corn might have difficulty in their own efforts. Before all is said and done, what is first described as blessing is a bit more complex than that. Knowledge plays a part, as does personal effort. Resources also contribute to the possibility. Connections grease the wheels. Gradually, what comes into focus is that there are fine lines between blessing, being fortunate, and privilege.

Perhaps the bulk of the problem is that we have accepted a version of the Gospel that equates participating in the kingdom of God with the expectation of prosperity and easy living rather than loving our neighbor or doing justice, loving kindness, and walking humbly. Or maybe, in our sincere efforts to be thankful, we give God direct credit for everything because that is what we think we are supposed to do, when, in fact, that is not the correct or at least the complete answer. While I am an advocate for a spirituality that embraces and notices divine presence in our world, this new round of puzzling over the idea of blessing leaves me with a few conclusions for myself. Feel free to consider them for yourself if you find them helpful.

I will try to view God as the center of my universe rather than myself as the center of God's world. That is to say, I should know up front that it is not all about me. That is not to say that each one is not precious to God, but neither is God my personal candy machine.

- Divine love does not mean that God should or will give me every last thing I ask for. I can ask, seek, and knock, but frankly, I do not always know how to pray. And if what I desire is bad for someone else whom God also loves, how is God to choose?
- If what feels like a blessing to me is hurtful to someone else, I should think carefully about how I speak about it. That is to say, I may feel blessed because the tornado missed my house, but if it wiped out my neighbor's home, perhaps I should not claim God was responsible?
- I will celebrate abundance when I have it and consider sharing it as I am able. Perhaps I am to be a conduit, not the final destination. After all, there is good biblical precedent for being a blessing to others.
- Innovation and effort are tremendous traits to claim, but we almost always stand on someone else's shoulders. Humility is usually a better choice than boasting about God's preferential treatment. The more we recognize our connectedness, perhaps the easier it is to share our bounty.
- Blessing is not to be equated with the acquisition of things. One valuable lesson from friendships with persons of different backgrounds and nations is their witness that joy and blessing are found among those who are poor as frequently (perhaps more frequently) as among the well-to-do.

So it would seem this year's corn crop exceeded my expectations in more ways than one. I have about had my fill. Take what you like, and leave the rest for someone else.

Query for Contemplation: How are the ideas of "blessing" and "privilege" related? How does a vision of equality for all persons alter your understanding of them?

Front Door Guests

Like most places, the small city of Paducah, Kentucky, holds reminders of times gone by tucked into a largely forward looking landscape. One site that captivates attention is a walk through the old Metropolitan Hotel. In the name of progress, it was nearly razed with other dilapidated eyesores in the neighborhood a few years ago. Today it is being restored, and visits there come complete with a narrated story by a volunteer portraying Maggie Steed, the original proprietor. The tour concludes with a piece of Maggie's homemade chess pie. That in itself is enough of a reason to stop by the hotel.

The Metropolitan Hotel is not a spectacular or elegant structure architecturally. It looks like many other houses from its era. Its power comes from the vision it represented and the story it tells. Built in the early 1900s, it is from a time when hotel chains didn't populate the roadside. McDonald's and Subways weren't stationed at interstate exits. Government-funded rest stops weren't available every fifty miles or so. Were you fortunate enough to find food and lodging, there was a chance that you weren't welcome to stay there—especially if you weren't white. If, by chance, admission was permitted for a person of color, there was a distinct possibility that they didn't receive the same level of service as others. Through what door do they enter the establishment? Where do they sit while eating? What restroom can they use? Travel was not easy.

At age twenty-four, a young widow named Maggie Steed managed to obtain a loan for the purpose of opening a hotel for Black people. The local bank resisted initially for the usual reasons but also, in part, because they assumed there was no market for such an establishment. Maggie insisted that wasn't true—that "people want a place where they could come in the front door." She was right. Over time, the likes of Louis Armstrong, BB King, Ike and Tina Turner, and Thurgood Marshall found rest and restoration within its walls as they traveled through the area. Those are names we all know. Their talents held wide appeal to a broad segment of the population. They are so well-known that some of us may never imagine the difficulties they encountered on their road to success.

"People want a place where they can come in the front door." Her words had no sooner left her mouth, and immediately, I understood it was true. On the dairy farm where I was raised, summer presented a need for a few extra hands over the course of a couple of weeks to help harvest silage to feed the cows. On those days, the workers usually ate lunch prepared by my grandmother. One day when she was unavailable, my mother cooked lunch instead. As the group sat down around the dining room table in our house, my father noticed an empty chair and realized one of the men was missing. Daddy found him, an elderly Black man, sitting outside on the steps with his plate in his lap. My dad called his name and said, "Come inside, and eat with the rest of us." The man answered, "No, thank you. I'm fine out here." My dad insisted, apparently already aware of the underlying problem, and said, "This is my house. It is my table. There is a place for you at it. Please come in, and eat with the rest of us."

I'll never forget what transpired next. As our friend joined the group at the table, one of the other men announced, "Well, if he is eating here I'm not sitting at this table." To this, my father responded, "Then you can leave, and don't bother coming back after lunch." We had one less driver that afternoon.

Being white, I have been spared the back-door experience based on race. Being from the rural South, I have occasionally felt rejection and barriers rooted in ridiculous attitudes about geography and language. Even so, I wouldn't equate my experience with theirs, other than to say what little experience I have had was enough to let me know the world shouldn't be ruled by such unfounded assumptions. Maggie's words stayed with me after the visit concluded. Why is it the sentence resonates so easily? What does that front door entrance symbolize?

Could it be rooted in the fact that front doors are made for receiving visitors? Some people go to great expense to create elaborate entrances, possibly to show their wealth but perhaps to set the mood and accentuate a sense of hospitality. Walking through it allows an opportunity for recognition and welcome by representatives of the home or business. Being allowed to pass through those doors is, itself, a sign of respect. Perhaps it is the owner, a family member, or an employee who is assigned that task, but the front door is where guests are expected to arrive. It is there that they are greeted, invited in, offered a seat and perhaps refreshment. On the other hand, back doors are often designated to receive packages and supplies. It is where we send deliveries whose arrival would be disruptive or out of character with the ambience of the front door. I have seen artsy signs that say something like, "Back door friends are the best." Perhaps the difference is those folks are already friends for whom questions of welcome and acceptance have been settled—not typically the case for passersby or when the designated door for use is based on something other than friendship.

Perhaps more so then than now, a place that takes you in also provides a sense of safety. In some cultures, a host's obligation of hospitality included protection as well as lodging or provision. Sleeping in meadows, beneath bridges, or over an exhaust grate on a cold evening, anywhere out in the wide open leaves a person exposed to whomever or whatever comes along. There is a lot more good in the world that we often recognize, but there is a fair amount of mischief as well. Who can get a good night's sleep if you need to sleep with one eye open? Within a home or hotel, there is no explicit promise of safety, but there is an implied commitment of a safe space. Electronic key systems or a night security guard help to create a perimeter of protection.

I can scarcely remember how hotels were located and reservations were made in the days before the internet put them within a few clicks reach, but on one trip to the Northeast, I'd booked a room outside of Philadelphia just over the New Jersey state line. It was a reputable budget chain brand, but when I arrived, the appearance suggested otherwise. Weeds growing where landscaping was expected, paint flaking off the building, hardly any cars in the parking lot, and a cast of assorted characters hanging out on the balcony all left me wondering what exactly I should expect. Safety seemed suspect in this case. After scoping out the joint, I followed my instincts and searched for different accommodations.

It turns out that welcome and safety are two prerequisites for a third thing we desire when we come through the front door: rest and renewal, whether that is through a good meal, a restful night, or even a few hours shopping (depending on what kind of front door welcomes you). It is difficult to relax when you know you aren't welcome. It is impossible to let go of pent-up stress or sleep the deep slumber that drives away fatigue when you feel unprotected and at risk. It is a challenge to engage in conversation, rekindling old friendships or forming new ones, when worry distracts us from being fully present in the moment. Being welcomed in the front door sends a clear message that, for better or worse, you have a place within this group.

Life gives us the challenge of balancing important values like freedom and private property with other worthy commitments like human rights and equality. When bias or prejudice relegates a person or group to a second-tiered status, things like welcome, safety, and relaxation evaporate like morning dew. There will always be things that make us distinct from one another, but we should consider if "distinct" is necessarily synonymous with "separate" or "different." I'm guessing it doesn't have to be so—at least not always—especially when an appreciation of creation allows us to enjoy its beauty and diversity, and we understand that our many distinctions are part of that whole. Whatever progress we have made on front-door matters, there is still plenty of work to be done.

I think Maggie Steed was on to something. For several good and right reasons, people want to come in the front door. It's a small way to help address some of life's important inequities. So think about putting out the welcome mat.

Query for Contemplation: When you consider those situations of inequality closest to you, do you find that you contribute to their creation or perpetuation? Can you identify changes of attitude or action on your part that would help create more equal relationships?

Fine Lines

The image of fine lines occupies my thoughts these days. I'm not thinking of geometry problems or lead sizes in pencils. Rather, it is the ever-so-slight boundaries in life that mark the separation of one perspective from another. They often seem harmless enough, but drift across one, and you may be surprised at the reaction it creates. Like being a computer geek in a biker bar or wearing shorts and a tank top to a black-tie affair, it quickly becomes clear that one of these is not like the others.

The topic of fine lines recently resurfaced a memory of working toward merit badges during my short-lived participation in the Boy Scouts. The badge being sought was for physical fitness or something similar, and one of the necessary activities focused on balance. A required task to earn the badge was to walk a certain distance balanced across a beam-like surface.

As it so happened, the attic space in our house was unfinished, so I spent a few hours attempting to walk across the exposed rafters in that space. In retrospect, that wasn't very smart. One misstep could have meant a foot crashing through the ceiling of the room beneath me. Thankfully, such an outcome was avoided.

The balancing act was easy enough while wearing shoes. Walking barefooted, on the other hand, was more of a challenge. Feet are uneven surfaces, of sorts, with arches, contours, and toes that squeeze or twitch.

Shoes have the advantage of a firm sole that doesn't react to a pinch or tickle. I don't remember too much more about that merit badge experience or any other for that matter, but from time to time, I remember the lessons learned about balance. It comes naturally but can be tricky. It is easier in some contexts than it is in others. To some degree, practice makes a difference. Master the act of balance, and you can navigate uncertain situations, walk upright in the best and worst of times, and avoid face plants in the most embarrassing of circumstances. I'm not a prime candidate for tightrope walking, but most days, I can at least put one foot in front of the other without falling.

The lesson about the importance of balance has been a good one but more for life than merit badges. I recently viewed a documentary called *Prohibition* by Ken Burns. Talk about an era with an absence of balance! It made the case that advocates of prohibition attempted to dictate behavior and a particular brand of morality. This, in itself, was out of character for a country that, by that stage, prided itself on freedom. From outspoken personalities like Carrie Nation to organized movements, this was an impressive accomplishment. Of course, there was pushback. Even with the passage of the eighteenth amendment prohibiting the manufacture, sale, and transportation of alcohol, a stiff drink could be found if a person knew where to look.

It is never easy to dictate or legislate morality. From stills to the speakeasy to alcohol by prescription to legal loopholes to protests by workers whose lives had long included alcohol, there was resistance to the imposition of temperance throughout the land. The documentary provided another reminder that there is a fine line between freedom and regulation. Most of us would acknowledge that abuse of alcohol can contribute to things like addiction, poverty, and domestic violence, but we would stop short of supporting the practice of prohibition. We could likely agree that an "anything goes" society is a hotbed for chaos, but we would probably have different opinions about what should be regulated or where the lines in the sand should be drawn. Depending on how we handle those moments, we may find ourselves balancing fine lines that separate collaborative action, spirited debate, protests, or more violent confrontations.

Thinking about this topic had already been brewing over the past four years, ever since the presidential election of 2016. Judi and I were traveling with a small group in Australia and New Zealand while votes were cast and counted that year. As results became known, the shock and despair that rippled through the group of travelers was noticeable, to say the least. We returned home to find many in our country were dismayed with a low morale and a doomsday perspective, while others were already mobilized to work for change. But that was only one side of the fine line. On the other side, some were quite pleased to have an outsider in the Oval Office who promised to drain the swamps of Washington, DC. The rancor between the two sides is what caught my attention. After all, someone loses every election. That wasn't a new outcome. And it wasn't our first rodeo.

I remember newsfeeds of those who protested in 2016. Again, in 2020, protests occurred. I support the right to protests, but never had I imagined we would witness fellow Americans storming our own Capitol.

Being a Quaker, I recognize that the majority isn't always correct simply because they outnumber their opposition. When that is the case, it is helpful if a minority prophetic witness can challenge us. That is different from choosing an oligarchy to govern the land. Crucial to navigating those moments is the freedom to express a differing point of view with the expectation that it will be heard with respect, even if disagreed with. Respectful disagreement allows us to work through our differences.

One solace during these trying times is a look back over history to see that the US has embraced, promoted, and survived despite such fractious behavior among our ancestors. I'm currently reading a book passed along by a niece called *Andrew Jackson and the Constitution*. Part of the author's point seems to be that US history is a history of generational regimes. The more successful one administration is, the more it guarantees a robust opposition by those left out of the power structure and who embody different ideals. That may not be a perfect description of what is facing our country at the moment, but it captures much of the cause of the underlying tensions. Those who feel they are being overlooked and ignored are taking the fight to those who wish to avoid trading places with them. Which group is which will, to some degree, depend on your vantage point when you survey the situation and make your assessment. We can expect that to continue until the day we create a system that leaves no one out.

I recall a college class called Dante and the Twentieth Century in which students chose theologians to read alongside *The Divine Comedy*. During my presentation of Paul Tillich's views of sin, grace, and perfection, the professor asked a question about freedom. I still remember my response: "We are free to live as we choose, but a person's freedom is curtailed when their decisions impinge on the freedom of another." I would still put that forth as a foundational presupposition in my thinking, but with a few more years of experience under my belt, I recognize how idealistic that statement is.

As an example, one of my neighbors owns two dogs. He has the right to own dogs. They spend much of their time indoors. While outside, it is perfectly acceptable for them to run loose in the yard. He is a good neighbor and has even gone the extra step of installing invisible fences so that the animals remain in the yard. Still, it is irritating to have the dogs stand at the fine line marked by the invisible fence and bark continuously at me when I walk down my own driveway to the mailbox. Two people exercising freedom within the boundaries of the life they've created for themselves. Each is well within their rights and the expectations of the law but with just a little friction on one side of the line, nonetheless. Imagine that situation but to the extreme, where parties involved aren't acquainted or certain rights are being violated or participants are simply tired of whatever it is that irks them. Balance and a healthy life together require a commitment to a few key ideals, recognizing value and worth in the other in spite of significant or even heated differences. It requires some skill at maintaining balance—walking those fine lines that separate us from one another on key points even as we still have more in common than not.

Perhaps qualifying for a merit badge that demonstrates our ability to maintain balance as we navigate these fine lines would be a helpful part of preparation for adulthood. It might save us from crashing through the ceiling later in life.

Query for Contemplation: What rights or liberties do you consider as fundamental that, upon inspection, might infringe on the liberties of others? Can you imagine a "third way" in which all parties mutually benefit from the change?

Toward a Testimony of Equality
Questions for Further Reflection

1. How does my access to basic needs and services compare with others in my geographic area? Are there inequities? If so, can I discern patterns or prejudices that contribute to these?
2. How is a commitment to equality evident in my friendships, affiliations, and communications? Do I identify areas where there is obvious work to be done in this area?
3. Quakers often begin statements about equality with a reference to "equality before God." What does a phrase like that mean? If I took that as my starting point, what would it require of me?
4. Does a testimony of equality require me to be more vocal about inequities that reinforce injustice or inhibit equal opportunities because of an uneven playing field?
5. When does privilege and good fortune among the faithful become problematic in a world where those supposedly equal before God are unequal among humanity?

Stewardship

Caring for and Caring about, Just Because

Stewardship encourages the judicious use of our gifts and resources as though we have none to waste, while generously sharing with others as though our abundance is unlimited. Responsible care and concern for all of creation, past, present, and future, is at the heart of this testimony.

Enough Already!

A visit to Star City, a once highly restricted area where cosmonauts trained for space missions, was included on the itinerary of a trip to Russia a few years ago. The premises appeared to be largely abandoned by that time, but Soviet-era architecture continued to set a serious tone for all who entered the area. The day's presenters were rightly proud of the research conducted there—and of their centrifuge. The TsF-18 centrifuge, used for cosmonaut physiology research and training at the Yuri Gagarin Cosmonaut Training Centre, was boastworthy. Its rotating arm measured fifty-nine feet in length and could simulate up to 30gs with a payload mass of 770 pounds. I don't fully understand that last sentence, except to know that it provides evidence of what they considered to be an extremely important part of the presentation: this is the biggest centrifuge in the whole world. If you don't believe the Russians, check the Guinness Book of World Records.

Why does it matter if it is the largest centrifuge so long as it serves it purpose? That seems like a fair question, but I honestly don't know the answer. A similar claim was made for a number of things we saw while visiting Russia. It was an obvious point of pride, perhaps even crucial to their identity and confidence. The attitude we encountered there fits neatly with a widely held sentiment that being the biggest and the best or having the most matters in this world (or even the smallest can be a point of pride so long as you are the "-est" of whatever you're representing). The thing at which you are biggest, smallest, or best doesn't have to be important or even interesting so long as it is "your thing." It may well become your claim to fame.

While verifying the TsF-18 centrifuge claim, I found these other "bests" also recorded by Guinness:

- Fastest woman biker—she rode eighteen thousand miles in 124 days. I know how I feel after riding a measly twenty-five miles. For her sake, I hope a lot of that route was downhill.
- Largest Hula Hoop spun by a woman—seventeen feet and one quarter inch. Not to be outspun, the men's record is seventeen feet, eight inches. I freely admit to being hula-challenged, especially when reading that the current record for continuous Hula-Hooping is one hundred hours, exceeding the previous record by twenty-five hours. My most recent effort with the Hula Hoop was decades ago. If I remember correctly, I was lucky to get more than three rotations before the hoop made a date with gravity to meet at the ground around my ankles.
- The longest lasting group hug—four Irish men hugged for thirty hours and one minute. I have to wonder if this one began after too many pints in a local pub. It is listed among a group of records that reportedly could be easily broken if you are looking to add your name to the book.
- Finally, for the strong among us, you might consider pursuing the most overhead presses of a person in one minute. The number is eighty-two. Think about it. That is faster than one repetition per second. At that rate, I hope the one being pressed doesn't have motion sickness issues. I don't know if there are minimum weight requirements for the person posing as a barbell, but I'd advise erring on the lighter side and practicing somewhere that provides a soft landing—just in case.

Those are interesting pastimes, and to each their own. Goals that motivate can be good things. Projects that invite focus and distract us from life's stresses contribute to our overall health. Hobbies that bring joy and entertainment help round out a full and satisfying life. Still, I often find myself wondering what the obsession is with being the best. Is enjoyment not possible otherwise? Don't misunderstand. This isn't a plea for mediocrity or lethargy. When I compete, I like to win! It begs the question, though, of why so many trivial things are turned into a contest with bragging rights at stake. I appreciate the desire to reach our full potential, but why is the urge to outdo everyone else added to the effort? Being the best I can be is one thing; being better than you is another. Why is that such a stimulant? Is it because competition is woven deeply into our DNA or our psyche?

On the other hand, I remember *The Ungame* from the 1970s. It was a noncompetitive game designed to promote communication rather than winning. Honestly, I hated it. For me, one thing worse than turning unimportant things into competitions was playing a game that nobody wins. Competition, winning, and (occasional) losing are fine. It is the obsession with being the best that puzzles me, where best is defined as "better than you." When that is the prevailing mindset, we are perpetually in one of two modes: seeking more so as to climb to the top of the scoreboard or defending our status so that no one dethrones us. On the playground or with board games, that may be harmless enough, but when those attitudes translate to real life, they establish patterns that encourage excessive accumulation and oppression, neither of which is ever fully satisfied. Gathering more is forever necessary if we are to progress; working against others helps prevent losing our place in the standings.

What would an alternative be? What if the goal was having or being "enough" rather than "best" or "most?" If that sounds like an absurd idea, consider the act of breathing. There is a case where we have learned to be content with enough breath. We are so confident that we have enough that we rarely think about it until something unusual like smoke and ash from wildfires darkens the sky and pollutes our air supply. We presume there is always enough for our needs and rarely worry about being deprived. Even if we did worry, it is not as though we could stockpile breath in our lungs, like toilet paper in our closets, so that we have extra in the house in case of a shortage. We can have too little breath, which is uncomfortable and even panic-inducing. But so far as I know, we can't store extra in our bodies to serve our needs, if say, we should run short next month (unless you count canisters of oxygen, perhaps).

Thinking about "enough" reminds me of a story in Exodus, where God provided food in the form of manna to the Israelites in the wilderness. After feeling deprived and facing a food shortage, a natural inclination is to stash some extra for the next time hunger strikes, like trying to sneak out a few leftovers from an all-you-can-eat buffet. With buffets, you can eat until you pop a button or two while you're there, but you can't take any leftovers with you. So it was with the manna. Part of the storyline in Exodus was that people were to gather only what was necessary for the day. That is to say, take only enough to meet one's immediate needs. No stockpiling allowed. It was an exercise in trusting divine provision. It goes against a frequent tendency to take advantage of the abundance of the moment to tide us over during the next shortage.

More and more, I find myself mulling over the idea of "enough" in contrast to "most" or best." It makes perfect sense but also feels slightly contrarian. Many social messages that influence us encourage always seeking more, but is "more" necessary? If that pursuit becomes an obsession with being the best or having the most, is that a wise choice for my overall well-being and aims in life? If it encourages a person to work longer hours or more years until, at some point, they no longer recognize their family, is that a healthy trade-off? Some of those excessive tendencies are for superficial and vain reasons. But other people's hectic lives are necessary for survival. It takes a lot of hours at minimum wage to cover the cost of living. Part of the challenge for some of us is to alter our values and reign in our choices; but another part is to give each other better alternatives to begin with.

I recently stumbled across a TED talk in which the speaker detailed his efforts to cap his corporation's profits while still meeting stakeholder expectations. He was committed to providing an acceptable return on their investments while also providing reasonably priced rental housing to a group being otherwise priced out of the neighborhood in which they worked. It was a logical set of steps to take once he had committed to the concept of "enough" rather than "most" as a guiding principle in his work. Many of us will never occupy a position where we make the kind of decision that will directly affect a wide portion of a neighborhood, but examples like that might inspire us to inspect our own areas of influence where seeking "enough" shifts our emphases and refreshes our lives while also improving others' chances for success. It may reduce stress or free energy for other pastimes—like Hula Hooping, for instance.

When asked, "How much money is enough?" John D. Rockefeller is reported to have said, "Just a little more." That means our work is never done. My childhood was spent working on the family farm. My adult work life primarily focused on serving as a pastor or an administrator. Each of those was an occupation where the work was never finished. Not really. There was always one more thing that could be done. A 24/7 commitment meant, even at leisure, you were on call if needed. To succeed in settings like those, one has to be content with having done enough for the time being. Accomplishing one more thing won't necessarily provide completion or satisfaction. One more work task won't likely be a game changer. In those the-work-is-never-done settings, one has to be willing to work hard but also to relax and play without succumbing to the pressure to do one more thing. And when it comes to money, honestly, it can be difficult to name a monetary figure that is enough. We can't foresee the future with clarity. Educated guesses are the best we can do, but we might fairly wonder if there isn't some level where more money doesn't translate to a better or happier life.

Why is the concept of enough so difficult to accept? Perhaps because we have never enjoyed a period in life in which we had enough. Money, food, love, freedom, and friends always seemed to run short so that the idea of enough has never occurred to us. We take what we can find and are always on the lookout for more. Or possibly even when we knew, on some level, that we had enough, something or someone pushed our buttons, and we felt not quite good enough or secure enough and mistakenly thought that "more" would alleviate that condition. Or maybe, from the earliest playground experience, it has seemed that someone has always been out to take what is yours, so it's important to protect it and be prepared for those worst-case scenarios. And especially when the ambition or aggression of others infringes on our peaceful efforts, the temptation to retaliate may rumble within us. There are multiple challenges to living as though we have enough, but I think it could be worth the risk. Perhaps we begin by asking things like:

- Am I driven by a desire or need to have more than I currently have? If so, why? Am I in fact suffering from a lack of enough or merely looking to add to my pile?
- What would change in my time, identity, and availability if I chose to seek "enough" rather than "more"?
- Do I have enough assets or support in my life to slow down and spend more time with the people I love, the pastimes I enjoy, and the community I cherish?
- If I don't love what I do, do I have "enough" to pivot in a new direction and pursue something that captures my heart?
- Do I have enough to share—be it wisdom, time, or something else—in ways that empower others to become enamored with "enough" as well?

Not until we have an idea of what is important and what is needed can we begin to contemplate releasing the idea that more and best are always preferable. Once we do, we may just discover that we have enough already.

Query for Contemplation: Are you possessed by a competitive edge that needs to be bigger and better than others? What drives that need?

When Cussing Just Won't Do

"For crying out loud!"

I heard myself muttering these words after the two-cycle engine of my small garden tiller refused to crank. I know it is in working order. A small engine shop nearby has a guy who can start anything. After servicing this tiller, he cranked it to demonstrate that he had performed the requested service. It responded to his very first pull of the starter rope, purring like a new engine; a few weeks later, when I was ready to till a section of the garden, it was not as accommodating for me. Apparently, this piece of equipment is as stubborn as its owner, working only when it is in the mood. The engine didn't start that day, but the experience did launch a thought process. What is the meaning of the phrase, "For crying out loud"? What is its origin?

According to the idioms origin website,[3] an American cartoonist is credited with introducing the phrase in the early twentieth century. It is an expression of exasperation, frustration, or disbelief. That much I knew because those are the only times it ever comes out of my mouth. But what does it mean? The website referred to it as a "minced oath," which was a new term for me. It describes the creation of a new phrase

---

3   Idiomorigins.org

that substitutes acceptable words for other words that we really want to say, but good manners or public opinion discourages their use. In this case, "for crying out loud" is supposedly a minced oath or euphemism that replaces "for Christ's sake." In effect, phrases like these are what we use when, for whatever reason, cussing just won't do.

My Southern-influenced vocabulary has a few such phrases circulating in reserve in case they are ever needed. "I'll be John Brown" is another one. Then there is "I'll be doggone." (Gone where, I always wondered.) I distinctly remember a gradeschool friend who was disciplined for using profanity when her language ran afoul of the school authorities. As a consequence, she tried to create what I now know is a minced oath. She wanted to vent her frustration and still be able to claim she'd not violated the rules. Her newly coined phrase included the words "summer peaches." She tried it out for a few days, but as far as I know, the expression never caught on.

Though not exactly a minced oath, perhaps "bless your heart" also belongs in a similar category. That phrase can be an actual expression of sympathy, but it can also be a subtle way of telling someone they're being naive. When someone blesses you that way, it takes careful listening to know if you're being comforted or ridiculed. Some will even describe a good verbal chewing out as "blessing you out" rather than "cussing you out." Either one is a good dressing down, but only one is acceptable in mixed company. A friend once remarked after reviewing a letter I'd drafted in response to a disagreeable communication from a denominational leader, "That's the nicest I have ever heard anyone called an S.O.B." Never let it be said that good manners need to interfere with speaking your mind. It seems we can contort rules and language in all sorts of ways that ease our consciences as we let off steam.

I wonder if, perhaps, that practice isn't at the root of a significant dilemma in our society. For fear of upsetting social convention, we soften what we say to the point that what is said loses its intended effect. When I read of yet another skirmish in the Middle East, I think, "Oh, for Pete's sake." Here we go again. (Or "for the love of Pete" or "in the name of

Pete"—again supposedly a substitute for "for Christ's sake" by replacing Christ with Peter.) It is easy to shake my head and move on to the next thought in the queue. Granted, I'm powerless to stop that conflict, but is there something more I could do than politely not swear about it? A prayer perhaps? A letter to a congressperson? Anything? How much violence persists around us, interrupting or destroying the lives of others in part because minced oaths allow us to maintain decorum and avoid speaking truthfully and forcefully to an issue?

If violence doesn't trouble us, what about various sorts of injustice? It is difficult for me to imagine any scenario in which a person should be suspected or mistreated simply because of their race or ethnicity. Imagine being pulled over for a bogus traffic violation just because of the color of your skin or the turban on your head. Envision opening your front door to discover derogatory graffiti spray-painted on your car, with no one ever held accountable for these misdeeds. I'd also not want for anyone to target me for retaliation because some of my professional colleagues' or personal associates' misbehavior. I'd rather not be denied a loan that I am perfectly capable of repaying just because the lending institution can discriminate without repercussions. Good grief! I can understand the decision to keep one's head down to avoid the spray, but is there something more we can do?

Greed is another social epidemic that makes me want to cuss a bit, but I know that is not a response that will change things. The desire to obtain a comfortable life with all the necessities and some of one's preferred luxuries is understandable, but few ever get around to asking questions like, "How much is enough? When do I not need more?" That is difficult to answer because of life's many uncertainties, but still, when the bulk of the world's wealth and resources are monopolized by a relative few, there is an elephant in the room. When the excess of a few deprives others of opportunities to achieve their own dreams, the system is broken. I recently watched a satirical 2019 movie from the UK called *Greed*. In graphic form, it demonstrates the evils of greed in memorable fashion. It easily leaves viewers disgusted. It might also nudge us to think about how we benefit from the system and consider ways we might resist it.

Sometimes, cussing just won't do—not because of social etiquette but because it has little effect. Perhaps there is a better way—better even than minced oaths and diluted criticism lobbed like under-filled water balloons that don't even burst upon impact. One creative example I encountered a few years ago involved a Friends meeting in New York City. It was shortly after the 9/11 tragedy. Fear and urges to retaliate were rampant, especially in the Big Apple, where the shock of it all registered close to home. Members of the Arab community in neighborhoods near the meetinghouse were apprehensive of walking outdoors.

Some Friends in the meeting zeroed in on a way to help. They offered to serve as escorts for members of this group. They would walk along with them from point A to point B to help ensure their safety. In doing so, they eased fear. They provided support. Plus, they gave witness to their commitment to build trust and friendship. I benefited from this effort one evening, enjoying a fabulous dinner in a Moroccan restaurant while individuals from both groups shared life and laughter as they described the relationships that had formed as a consequence of this effort. That response was a darn sight better than shaking heads and mumbling muted expletives about how things need to change.

A few years ago, while looking for resources to use in a leadership course, I found a book titled *Walk Out, Walk On*. It told the stories of communities that took the initiative to leave behind limiting beliefs and practices, working instead to build healthy communities, tackling complex problems like homelessness, poverty, and public safety. It is the kind of response that can occur when a group determines no one else is coming to fix the problem for them. If there is to be a better world, they would need to be part of the solution. Glory be! You have to wonder why an idea like that doesn't garner more support.

For crying out loud! It is the easy, impulsive first response. The world is filled with causes for exasperation. There are numerous reasons for anger to abound. It may even feel like it is time to throw decorum to the wind and dip into the four-letter word collection. But the deeper truth is that, if we want a better world, we have work to do—for ourselves, our communities, and our next generation. Clearly, this is time when cussing just won't do.

Query for Contemplation: Your minced oaths may well identify the points of frustration calling for attention in your life. Listen to your words. They may suggest the right next area for you to address. Where are your words calling you to act?

Pimento Cheese? Really?

So what is pimento cheese, anyway? That is not a question I had dwelt on until it invaded my search for cheeseburger excellence. Until then, it was mostly a faint memory from my youth. Among the items usually kept in our family's refrigerator was a plastic container filled with a creamy spread. It was light orange in color, almost like a dreamsicle or sherbet that had fallen on hard times. Tiny red specs were mixed with small chunks of grated cheese and mayonnaise. At our house, it usually wound up as the innards of a sandwich, though the adventurous would occasionally slap some on a cracker or maybe even a piece of celery. In my food hierarchy, pimento cheese ranked below all the meat sandwiches but well above tuna or egg salad.

Years had passed since I'd thought of pimento cheese, but one day, a container of it caught my eye in the supermarket, so we bought one for old time's sake. Its return to our refrigerator also brought a curiosity about the cheese's origin. Lots of folks assume it originated in the South in the early 1900s, but it seems to have been sold all across the country in groceries at that time. It was made from a soft white French cheese called Neufchâtel mixed with red peppers. It may have been to World War I what SPAM was to World War II, as it was a cheap way to feed an army. Grated cheese, mayo, and sliced pimiento peppers are the main ingredients in every recipe I've located. Some chefs may reduce the mayo in favor of cream cheese or add a few other spices to give it their own signature flavor, but as to the question of what is pimento cheese, that is it. We made sandwiches with our supermarket purchase. They were tasty enough, triggered some enjoyable reminiscing, and that was that. Until, that is, a chance encounter last summer.

It was a hot June day on the Blue Ridge Parkway, and Judi and I were providing SAG (support and gear) wagon support for my sister as she biked the parkway. She would take off in the mornings with a destination in mind. We'd explore sites in the area, staying nearby in case she needed us, meeting her at the endpoint at a designated time. When lunch time rolled in, Judi and I happened upon a spot called Mabry Mill, located in a region known as the Meadows of Dan. According to their website, the mill itself was completed around 1908. It was the first of a few small businesses operated by Ed and Lizzie Mabry. Many of these have been preserved or reconstructed, making for a nice stop if you are in the area and need to stretch your legs. And they have a restaurant.

One of the items promoted on the menu is the Wheel Burger. It is described as a ground beef patty topped with choice of lettuce, tomato, onion, and mayonnaise covered with house-made pimento cheese and topped with crispy bacon on a Bavarian pretzel roll. I enjoy a good pretzel roll as a variation on a standard hamburger bun. In my humble opinion, bacon can improve just about anything. But pimento cheese was a new twist on the cheeseburger for me, so of course, I had to try it. I'd had it as the main ingredient of a sandwich and as a spread on finger foods but never as the main cheese featured on a burger.

Frankly, it seemed like a stretch. I wasn't sure what to expect. Plus, pimento cheese is made with mayonnaise, so isn't it redundant to add mayo as a condiment to the burger? Over time, I've learned never to criticize a cook until you've tried their cooking; even then, proceed with caution, and if possible, wait until they are in the other room. So I ordered the Wheel Burger.

I'd be lying if I said it was love at first bite. It was a bit like seeing your boss at the movies or the minister at the supermarket. You recognize the person, but something is out of kilter. Seeing them in a different context requires a slight adjustment on your part—like slumping down in the theater seat to avoid your boss's gaze or putting on your most virtuous walk in case the minister meets you on aisle four. The first bite gave me that kind of pause, but after a second and third bite, the pimento spread and I became reacquainted, and I could appreciate the flavor it brought to this dish.

I had to wonder how this cheeseburger combo came about. Maybe it's an example of "necessity is the mother of invention"—as the burger cooked on the grill, someone who craved a cheeseburger learned the cupboard was bare except for this cheese spread, so it was this or nothing. Or its discovery could have been a happy accident, the way Reese's Peanut Butter Cups once advertised the introduction of peanut butter to chocolate. Someone unintentionally dropped a dollop of pimento cheese on a freshly cooked burger, and the rest is history. Perhaps it was the result of culinary creativity that proved to be delicious. Quite possibly, it was just someone who really loved pimento cheese spread who could think of nothing better than putting two good friends, hamburger and pimento cheese, together for a mealtime treat. Whatever the origin, it is here to stay, immortalized at the Mabry Mill restaurant as one feature of a historical and regional tribute.

I appreciate those who are bold enough to try new things and, when the results meet their approval, share them with a wider audience. Sampling the things others treasure can help us understand the person as well as broaden our horizons. It reminds me of a visit many years ago to a steakhouse near Raleigh, North Carolina. I was feasting on a complimentary cheesespread with crackers and clearly enjoying it. The server asked if I wanted blue cheese as my salad dressing. I thought that was presumptuous of her and answered, "Heavens no! I hate blue cheese. I'll have ranch please. By the way, the cheese in this crock is delicious. What is it, and can I buy some to take home?" Her reply? "It's blue cheese. That's why I thought you'd want it for a salad dressing." So, I changed my order. Somewhere I'd formed the mistaken notion that I didn't like blue cheese. It only took one opportunity of getting to know it on its own terms to appreciate it fully. Not all changes of heart come so quickly, but lessons like those, even if slightly embarrassing in the moment, teach me the value of sampling new experiences and opportunities.

It brings to mind a favorite verse from Psalm 34:8, "Taste and see that the Lord is good." That can be read as an imperative, directing us to what is eternal and true, which it does. But it also implies that experimentation is what convinces us of the goodness. There are so many positive experiences and amenities in our lives thanks to two things: someone shared their new discovery, and we eventually got around to trying it ourselves. Take swimming, for instance. Who was the first person to get into water over their head and figure out how to paddle without sinking? Thank goodness somebody taught me. Or think of plumbing. Whoever popularized indoor plumbing has sure made life easier, though as you might expect, for a while, some insisted on clinging to their outhouses. Not all new ideas work out, but let's face it, if we weren't willing to risk something different from time to time, we'd all still be on a diet of milk and baby food.

So next time you're in the mood for a burger, try one with pimento cheese. You may discover a new favorite.

Query for Contemplation: Consider how being a good steward of resources includes openness to letting go of prior assumptions and the sampling or even embrace of new ideas and practices.

The Risk of Kindness

If you look up the word "gullible" in the dictionary, do not be surprised if you find my picture provided as an example. I have a tendency to give people the benefit of the doubt until they prove to be untrustworthy. Some call it being attentive, compassionate, or big-hearted. Gullible may be the unvarnished description. I prefer to think of it as kindness.

Given the option to do a kind thing or nothing at all, I often do the kind thing even if it is not necessary. Honestly, this practice is mildly perturbing. I am so tired of manipulative appeals from nonprofits that siphon off questionable amounts of gifts for "administrative overhead." Many of us are understandably both weary and wary of appeals for assistance (i.e., television commercials, glossy direct mail, personal requests on streets), but those are not states of being I am willing to let rule the day. Human need and the potential to make a difference capture my attention. I imagine that is why I can easily make a list of moments when I feel something stir within me that causes me to think that, perhaps, I am being nudged to care in a way that lightens another's burden.

These experiences have prompted me to reflect from time to time on the value of kindness. What is not to like about kindness? It is soft, gentle, and helpful. It is not necessarily costly, though that varies according to the gesture made. But as it has been observed in folk wisdom handed down, "It is more difficult to be kind than clever." At a minimum, I take that to mean the first challenge to kindness is an internal one where we must overcome the urge to outsmart, outfox, or outdo others for our own gain, choosing instead to be collegially or cooperatively helpful.

If we are fortunate enough to prevail in that internal skirmish, it is important to recognize that kindness requires more than one's intention. It is a bit like the old joke about the scout who helped the elderly person across the street. It was intended as an act of kindness, only the elderly person did not want to cross the street. Just because we intend something to be kind does not guarantee that it will be received that way. During one period of our marriage, as part of the division of labor, I washed and dried the laundry while Judi folded and put it away. One day in preparation, I carried clothes to the laundry room, dumped them on the floor and sorted things into piles. Whites. Colors. Reds. When I returned to start the first load of laundry, all the items had been returned to one huge pile. I asked Judi, "Did you put all of these items into one pile?"

She responded in the affirmative, obviously happy with her good deed.

"Why would you do that?" I wanted to know.

She said, "I was being kind and helpful."

Well, not really. Unsorting sorted laundry does not pass the kindness test—at least not on that day. It was a nice thought, and I appreciated her intent, but some acts of kindness just aren't helpful, no matter how good-intentioned they are. After a good laugh, I teasingly asked if there was anything else she intended to help with that I should know about.

One would not think that kindness could be so complicated, but it can be. Things like lack of understanding the other's predicament, cultural differences that lead to miscommunication, or unintended offense. There are numerous reasons why it is easier to ignore it all and avoid the headaches. But on the flip side, sometimes we discover that, over time, the absence of kindness creates deep scars in a relationship. I knew a couple who had built a seemingly successful, strong household over many years together. One day, the husband announced that he had filed for divorce, having found someone else with whom he desired to share his life. The wife was understandably crushed and furious. A good attorney negotiated that the wife would receive 90 percent of their assets in the divorce settlement, should they proceed. With that, she felt certain that her husband would not leave her. There was no way he would walk away from those assets. She had won this battle and saved the marriage. Only she had not. The husband agreed to take only a 10 percent portion without protest, which of course raised the question, "Why? What is it about this other relationship that would motivate relinquishing 90 percent of one's assets?" The response was memorable. The other person was kind. She was gentle. She took time for simple things like talking at the end of the day and holding his hand.

There is usually more to a story than a third party ever knows. Without supporting either side, what stayed with me from those conversations was the power and importance of kindness. Without it, seemingly solid relationships can crack and crumble. With it, a person's world takes on a wholly different tenor, potentially leading to a transformation of attitude and demeanor.

I have witnessed the impact of kindness upon people, especially in children. Those who primarily hear criticism and ridicule often internalize those messages to the point that their self-esteem is chipped away, and their demeanor is dampened. Into that downward spiral, the introduction of just one affirming voice can have an amazing influence. Like light at the end of the tunnel, it provides a guide point toward which the child hastens. Temperament and work ethic alike can change; they may even begin to excel in talents and abilities they had never before exhibited.

The effect of kindness is not limited to children, and we are fools if we believe that adults do not respond similarly. For instance, it is true with adults in the workplace. In the field of leadership studies, a growing number of voices recognize that so-called soft skills like kindness are beneficial to organizational health and do not necessarily compromise organizational objectives or undermine a leader's authority.

While one small kindness will not resolve all the world's aches and pains, it can be the first step toward new perspectives and possibilities. A few years ago, there was a trend referred to as "random acts of kindness." These were sometimes small acts, like paying for the fast food order of the car behind you. They could be not-so-small acts as well, like taking an extra job to anonymously pay bills of a family member or generously paying for the Christmas lay-away purchases for all customers at a store. The hope was that one small act would inspire another, multiplying their effectiveness. In fact, there is now a Random Acts of Kindness Foundation, which promotes a day or even a week for practicing random acts of kindness.

I think random acts of kindness are great. They are inspirational; I like to imagine that they send ripples of goodwill into the community. But there is a problem if this is our only strategy. Random acts leave large gaps between experiences of kindness. So these days, I want to advocate for something like regularized acts of kindness or continual acts of kindness. Who knows? A bit of kindness spread widely might help take the edge off of the highly reactive, defensive mood that is prevalent in our society.

It may well be that I am indeed gullible to think that kindness can be such a leaven in the loaf, but I prefer to think there is a divine prompt behind these apparently gullible actions. Kindness is more than merely being nice; it is an opportunity to participate in the work of the Spirit among us. It is a chance to be a good steward in the moment, using what I have to assist others in a moment of need. Kindness is not the least I can do; it ranks among the best that I can do for another. Whenever I experience a time of need, I know how valuable it is to find someone who will respond to my story. Even with the possibility of being hustled from time to time, I am of the opinion that kindness is worth the risk.

Query for Contemplation: As you visualize ways you care for the world you inhabit, what risks are you willing to take that would gift kindness and generosity to those you encounter?

Toward a Testimony of Stewardship

Questions for Further Reflection

1. If I imagine myself as a caretaker of the earth rather than merely an occupant or consumer, how does that affect my self-image and attitude?
2. How do I view my assets? Are they for my benefit alone, or are there ways they can benefit a wider network of people?
3. What decisions could I make that would reduce the amount of waste I discard?
4. Do my decisions about purchases and accumulation of resources reflect my concern for caring for the earth?
5. Identify a local project where a small collective effort could have a restorative effect in your community and provide an opportunity for a collaborative project.

Conclusion: A Life of Ongoing Encounter, Reflection, and Deep Joy

A recent online post asked readers for their definition of spirituality. Most responses moved toward the ephemeral. They were nicely stated, reaching beyond this so-called lower realm toward the heights to which they aspired. A slight problem, though, is that, if these definitions had been pairs of pants, I wouldn't have known where to put in my leg; that is to say, their practical usefulness escaped me. Often, when we turn our minds to spiritual things, we so worry about missing the mark that beautiful statements yield little real help.

In contrast to that, a friend remarked some years ago that I had an "earthy spirituality." While I'm not sure exactly what was intended by that comment, I chose to interpret it as a compliment. I prefer a spirituality that is understandable and useful. I need a seven-days-a-week, wash-and-wear faith that is not afraid of rolling in the mud. It is not that I deliberately set out in search of a muck pit; I just want to be able to wade in as needed.

Testimonies provide just that sort of assistance. As North Star principles, they may appear obvious in retrospect, but they probably were not immediately so evident. They arise out of worship but also from addressing life's challenges. Having encountered a dilemma or an issue, time was taken to reflect on the matter at hand and to consider options available. Within that consideration was also an opportunity to listen for the guidance of the Spirit—to be led toward a faithful response. The ultimate outcome may not have been immediate or certain, but testing over a period of time gave the evidence needed to confirm this was a good and faithful response.

Life can be fragmented and hectic. Even when that is not the case, much of it encourages quick decisions that lack depth. For instance if a busy schedule and hunger collide, resulting in my being in a fast food drive-through, I need to be ready to order when my turn arrives. A prompt response on my part keeps the line moving, helps everyone get served, and addresses both my schedule and my hunger. But if I were to pause long enough to consider the nutritional value of that meal and considered details like sodium intake compared with recommended daily allowances, would I still make the same decision? And if I had had that conversation with myself at an earlier time rather than in a rushed moment and arrived at the conclusion that this was not a suitable lunch for me, might I have made other arrangements—either follow a different schedule or pack a lunch?

With a small dose of intrigue and reflection, what first appears to be an insignificant encounter in a regular day can open layers of conversation and insight—an exchange with a vendor at a tourist stop, a walk through a town's central park, or savoring a new combination of condiments on a burger, for instance. Moments like these are frequently rich with meaning. When we are more attentive to the event and go deeper into the moment, we can not only better appreciate what has gone into creating this experience, but we also can begin to identify principles and commitments that make their occurrence possible. The mundane becomes a gateway to conversations with the Divine, as daily experience becomes worship lived on full display within the details of life. Those conversations, in turn, begin to highlight trusted values or new openings. They make space to explore the hows and whys of our joys and pains. We become clearer about what matters to us—and with that, these encounters have led us to the threshold of the things that rank as our own testimonies. This proves to be one of the most precious gifts we can give to ourselves, because with knowledge of them in hand, we can fashion lives that align with the things we most deeply value. Imagine spending your time devoted to what matters most to you, especially when it has been identified and shaped by the work of the Spirit.

What rises to the level of a testimony for you may be different than the SPICES represented here, and that is absolutely fine. What's important is that we each do the work necessary to identify the values and principles by which we wish to order our lives. Personally, I find that these Quaker testimonies provide a tremendously helpful foundation.

For instance, simplicity perhaps sounds old-fashioned, but it offers so much more. With coffee served in such a variety of options these days, who orders a plain cup of joe? How boring and unimaginative is that? Why settle for plain and simple when there is razzle and dazzle to be had? But which one to choose? Life presents so many possible choices for using my time; I can spend days perusing the menu. But not all options are equal, and while many are constructive in their own right, they consume time better spent elsewhere. They may even complicate my ability to focus on that which is most important for me. Simplicity combats that tendency. It works to identify my core commitments and makes it easier to stay true to what matters. Its tendency to see through and strip away needless, superfluous trappings makes for a cleaner, fresher run through life.

In turn, simplicity complements peace to some degree. Eradicating crabgrass from a lawn may be easier than ridding the world of obstacles to peace, but I think peace is more obtainable once simplicity is rooted in your heart. Initially, a less aggressive pace and shorter list of must-have items lengthens my fuse because accumulation is no longer my primary driving force. Peace has a better chance of flourishing if I'm not already burning when I arrive at the fire. Amazingly, a peaceful inner disposition filters through my being. Not only is my fuse not lit, but I'm less likely to be the gasoline that sends your flame raging toward the sky.

Admittedly, peacemaking is tiring work. It requires choosing to be less reactive. It insists on dealing with difficult issues with resolution as its goal. It necessitates listening and caring about the perspectives of others. It means letting some things pass by when, in fact, I'd like to take a swing at it. Equally important and sometimes exceedingly difficult, it will require that I be open to finding a new, third way to bridge the gap between differing opinions. However challenging it is, peace holds out the promise of a safer world in which to make our home and create supportive clusters of people.

Perhaps peace is so elusive because other testimonies are missing from our lives. For instance, even though integrity winds up in the middle of the SPICES list, it is frequently my starting point if I'm forced to rank the testimonies. It is as important to character and relationships as a foundational cornerstone is to a building's stability. Integrity provides a trustworthy footing upon which other structures can be built and supported. Ultimately, the issue is one of reliability. In a home, I prefer a floor that doesn't give way or a roof that doesn't leak. In relationships, I desire a similar kind of consistency. I grew up in a family that taught a person was only as good as their word, and their word should be their bond. That perspective isn't as prevalent as it once was, but for better or worse, it still lives within me. With people, I want to be able to trust the other rather than worry about being deceived or taken advantage of. I find it most difficult to have patience or work with individuals and processes where that kind of integrity is absent. Why? Without it, there is a lack of trustworthiness and reliability.

Imagine the difference integrity makes in the creation of a community. What is a community but a group of individuals who have started to develop some level of intimacy in their relationships? They have begun to share their personal stories. They have recognized shared visions and compatibility in one another. Integrity contributes to the health and stability of a community because the relationships are built upon reliable foundations.

Many days, I could pass for a lone wolf. I enjoy solitude and some distance from life's busyness. But some occasions remind me I need more. Like the day I discovered two huge ash trees had fallen and blocked my driveway. As I set out for what proved to be several hours of chainsawing, I recalled images from the surrounding Amish community where, for certain projects, most of the community turns out to help accomplish the task. I may not have needed a whole community for the trees, but a few more able bodies would have been a bonus. At certain times, life is more manageable with a network of support. Whether in the form of physical assistance, collective wisdom, or simple fellowship, the companionship and accompaniment of a community provide amazing support along the journey—and not just for life's unwanted surprises.

Particularly in those communal situations but also true when dealing with strangers, a testimony like equality can be a game changer. It can be a difficult pill to swallow if a competitive culture or an attitude of superiority has surrounded you all of your life. A mindset like that convinces us that much of our self-worth is tied to being better than others. Being smarter, faster, stronger, prettier—a multitude of categories ranks us and sets us in perpetual competition. Blown to unhealthy extremes, it can feed resentment or even seething anger if the gap of inequality grows too large. Equality helps fill those chasms and heal those wounds because it refuses to give power to these sorts of distinctions. Instead, it recognizes "that of God" in the other and chooses to foster a connection built on that equal starting point. Incredibly, something that simple can open the door for conversation, mutual learning, and even friendship. Equality is like a rich compost promoting vigorous growth in the garden of community.

Whether you are alone or within a group, stewardship injects a combination of gratitude, caring, and forward vision to our activities.

Gratitude helps us recognize that our opportunities result as much from the accomplishments of those who have gone before us as from our own efforts. Care, because we understand that however vigorous our life may be, we are merely passing through this earth. That which we have inherited, we will eventually leave the next generation. During our time here, while we benefit from the contributions of others, stewardship teaches us to be mindful of what we are leaving for those who follow us. Alongside a pursuit of success and pleasure, concepts like contribution and consequence factor into our decisions. We cease to be takers only, intending to give back so that others may also succeed.

There is no ideal number of testimonies, but it should be becoming obvious that they share similarities with a jigsaw puzzle. They are interlocking pieces. However intriguing one is, it gains strength when surrounded by others. Initially, it may be difficult to understand how they fit together, what they add to the picture, or even what is impossible when they are lacking. With time, we learn how they connect and catch a glimpse of the picture they represent. Together, the testimonies we choose provide a whole system by which we evaluate what is before us, dream of what we might become, and navigate our next steps. In the histories and treatises, they may sound abstract and larger than life, but honestly, they are best when they rise from our reflection within the daily experiences of our life—in solitude and together.

www.ingramcontent.com/pod-product-compliance
Lightning Source LLC
Chambersburg PA
CBHW011951150426
43195CB00019B/2896